Edición Segunda

Manual completo de los verbos en INGLÉS

Prof. Jaime Garza Bores

McGraw·Hill

New York   Chicago   San Francisco   Lisbon   London   Madrid   Mexico City
Milan   New Delhi   San Juan   Seoul   Singapore   Sydney   Toronto

Library of Congress Cataloging-in-Publication Data

Garza Bores, Jaime.
    Manual completo de los verbos en ingles / Jaime Garza Bores.
        p.   cm.
    ISBN 0-07-144496-3
    1. English language—Textbooks for foreign speakers—Spanish.   2. English
language—Verb—Handbooks, manuals, etc.   I. Title.

PE1129.S8G358   2005
428.2'461—dc22   2004055986

Originally published by Editorial Diana and Editorial Universo

    11 12 13 14 15   QFR/QFR   1 5 4 3 2 1

ISBN 0-07-144496-3

McGraw-Hill books are available at special quantity discounts to use as premiums and
sales promotions, or for use in corporate training programs. For more information, please
write to the Director of Special Sales, Professional Publishing, McGraw-Hill, Two Penn
Plaza, New York, NY 10121-2298. Or contact your local bookstore.

This book is printed on acid-free paper.

Contenido

Preface

Designed with the needs of Spanish speakers in mind, *Manual completo de los verbos en inglés* presents the main features of the English verb system in a single, compact volume.

In it you will find:

- A list of the most common regular verbs in English.

- A complete list of irregular verbs in English, grouped according to pattern. This special feature allows irregular verbs to be easily learned in related groups. Examples illustrate the verbs in context, and notes give important information on the meaning and usage of the different forms.

- A complete list of all auxiliary verbs in English, along with complete examples of all the tenses they form and notes explaining their meaning and usage.

This unique book is the perfect way to learn English verbs quickly, practically, and economically!

Prólogo

Específicamente diseñado para los hispanoparlantes, *Manual completo de los verbos en inglés* reúne las características de los verbos y ofrece múltiples ejemplos de los mismos en un solo tomo.

El lector encontrará:

- Los verbos regulares más comunes.

- Los verbos irregulares catalogados según sus formas; de esta manera se aprenderán más fácilmente.

- Ejemplos y notas que ofrecen información valiosísima sobre el uso apropiado de los verbos.

- Los verbos auxiliares con cuadros de construcción que muestran cómo se emplean.

Este manual es el instrumento perfecto para aprender a manejar los verbos rápidamente.

AUXILIAR *TO BE*

Tiempo en presente	*Tiempo en pasado*
AM (soy, estoy)	
IS (es, está)	*WAS* (era, estaba, estuvo)
ARE (son, están)	*WERE* (eran, estaban, estuvieron)

Observe cómo emplear el auxiliar. *TO BE* (ser o estar) en sus tiempos presente y pasado con el verbo *to write* (escribir) en su forma *ING* (escribiendo). Note las expresiones de tiempo *now* (ahora) y *yesterday* (ayer), así como los pronombres *I* (yo), *he* (él) y *they* (ellos).

1.	I	*AM*	writing a letter *now*
2.	He	*IS*	writing a letter *now*
3.	They	*ARE*	writing a letter *now*
4.	I	*WAS*	writing a letter *yesterday*
5.	They	*WERE*	writing a letter *yesterday*

TRADUCCIÓN

1. Yo estoy escribiendo una carta ahora
2. Él está escribiendo una carta ahora
3. Ellos están escribiendo una carta ahora
4. Yo estuve escribiendo una carta ayer
5. Ellos estuvieron escribiendo una carta ayer

NOTA: Empléase *IS*, en *he, she, it* y *ARE* en *you, we, you, they*. Empléase *WAS* en *I, he, she, it* y *WERE* en *you, we, you, they*.

Nótese ahora la partícula negativa NOT después de *am*, *is, are, was* y *were* para formar las negaciones en presente y en pasado.

I	*am*	NOT	writing a letter *now*
He	*is*	NOT	writing a letter *now*
They	*are*	NOT	writing a letter *now*
I	*was*	NOT	writing a letter *yesterday*
They	*were*	NOT	writing a letter *yesterday*

En las preguntas *am, is, are, was, were* se anteponen a los pronombres *I, he, they.*

AM	I writing a letter *now?*
IS	he writing a letter *now?*
ARE	they writing a letter *now?*
WAS	I writing a letter *yesterday?*
WERE	they writing a letter *yesterday?*

CUADRO SINÓPTICO DEL VERBO *TO BE*

PRESENTE   *PASADO*

Afirmativo	Afirmativo
I AM	I WAS
You ARE	You WERE
He ⎫ She ⎬ IS It ⎭	He ⎫ She ⎬ WAS They ⎭
We ⎫ You ⎬ ARE They ⎭	We ⎫ You ⎬ WERE They ⎭

Negativo	Negativo
I AM ⎫ You ARE He ⎫ She ⎬ IS ⎬ NOT It ⎭ We ⎫ You ⎬ ARE They ⎭ ⎭	I WAS ⎫ You WERE He ⎫ She ⎬ WAS ⎬ NOT It ⎭ We ⎫ You ⎬ WERE They ⎭ ⎭

Interrogativo	Interrogativo
AM I?	WAS I?
ARE you?	WERE you?
IS ⎰ he? ⎱ she? ⎱ it?	WAS ⎰ he? ⎱ she? ⎱ it?
ARE ⎰ we? ⎱ you? ⎱ they?	WERE ⎰ we? ⎱ you? ⎱ they?

AUXILIARES DEL INTERROGATIVO PARA EL TIEMPO PRESENTE Y PASADO DE TODOS LOS VERBOS EN INGLÉS

(excepto *to be*: ser o estar; *can*: poder; *must*: deber)

Tiempo en presente	Tiempo en pasado
DO { Interrogativo para: I, you, we, you, they	DID. { Interrogativo para: I, you, we, you, they
DOES { Interrogativo terceras personas: he, she, it	DID { Interrogativo terceras personas: he, she, it

Observe el empleo de *DO* y *DOES* para preguntar en tiempo presente; y *DID* para hacer preguntas en tiempo pasado. Advierta asimismo el verbo en su forma simple *(write)* en el pasado interrogativo (3 y 4) puesto que *DID* basta para expresar dicho pasado.

1. DO   you *write* many letters *every day?*

2. DOES he *write* many letters *every day?*

3. DID   you *write* many letters *yesterday?*

4. DID   he *write* many letters *yesterday?*

TRADUCCIÓN

1. ¿Escribe usted muchas cartas todos los días?
2. ¿Escribe él muchas cartas todos los días?

3. ¿Escribió usted muchas cartas ayer?
4. ¿Escribió él muchas cartas ayer?

NOTA: El pasado de los verbos se emplea únicamente en la forma afirmativa: I *wrote a letter yesterday* (Yo escribí una carta ayer).

AUXILIARES DEL PRESENTE Y PASADO NEGATIVO
PARA TODOS LOS VERBOS EN INGLÉS

(excepto *to be*: ser o estar; *can*: poder; *must*: deber)

Presente negativo	Pasado negativo
DO NOT (para: *I, you, we, you, they*)	DID NOT (para: *I, you, you, they*)
DOES NOT (terceras personas: *he, she, it*)	DID NOT (terceras personas: *he, she, it*)

Observe el empleo de NOT después de *do, does* y *did* en las negaciones en tiempo presente y pasado.
Nótese el verbo en su forma simple *(write)* en el pasado negativo (3 y 4) después de *did* NOT, puesto que esto basta para expresar dicho pasado.

1. I   *do*   NOT *write* many letters   *every day*
2. HE *does* NOT *write* many letters   *every day*

3. I   *did*   NOT *write* many letters *yesterday*
4. He *did*   NOT *write* many letters *yesterday*

TRADUCCIÓN

1. Yo no escribo muchas cartas todos los días
2. Él no escribe muchas cartas todos los días

3. Yo no escribí muchas cartas ayer
4. Él no escribió muchas cartas ayer

NOTA: El pasado de los verbos se emplea únicamente en la forma afirmativa: I *wrote* a letter yesterday (yo escribí una carta ayer).

10

PATRÓN DE CONSTRUCCIÓN DEL TIEMPO PRESENTE EMPLEANDO EL VERBO TO WRITE

Tiempo presente: *WRITE (S)* = escribo, escribes, escribe, escribimos, escriben.

Afirmativo	Interrogativo			Negativo		
I write	*DO*	I	write?	I *DO*	NOT	write
You write	*DO*	you	write?	You *DO*	NOT	write
He write*S*	*DOES*	he	write?	He *DOES* NOT write		
She write*S*	*DOES*	she	write?	She *DOES* NOT write		
It write*S*	*DOES*	it	write?	It *DOES* NOT write		
We write	*DO*	we	write?	We *DO*	NOT	write
You write	*DO*	you	write?	You *DO*	NOT	write
They write	*DO*	they	write?	They *DO*	NOT	write

Para conjugar cualquier otro verbo en tiempo presente (excepto *to be*: ser o estar, *can*: poder y *must*: deber), síganse los mismos patrones empleados con *to write*. Es decir, los que se destacan con letras mayúsculas: S, DO, DOES, DO NOT y DOES NOT. Por lo tanto, al conjugar otro verbo regular o irregular empléense dichas mayúsculas en la misma posición y orden en que aparecen con *to write*.

PATRÓN DE CONSTRUCCIÓN DEL TIEMPO PASADO EMPLEANDO EL VERBO *TO WRITE*

Tiempo pasado: *WROTE* = escribí, escribió, escribimos, escribieron.

Afirmativo	Interrogativo	Negativo
I wrote	*DID* I write?	I *DID* NOT write
You wrote	*DID* you write?	You *DID* NOT write
He wrote	*DID* he write?	He *DID* NOT write
She wrote	*DID* she write?	She *DID* NOT write
It wrote	*DID* it write?	It *DID* NOT write
We wrote	*DID* we write?	We *DID* NOT write
You wrote	*DID* you write?	You *DID* NOT write
They wrote	*DID* they write?	They *DID* NOT write

Para conjugar cualquier otro verbo en tiempo pasado (excepto *to be*: ser o estar, *can*: poder, *must*: deber), síganse los mismos patrones empleados con *to write*. Es decir, los que se destacan con letras mayúsculas: *DID* y *DID* NOT.

Por lo tanto, al conjugar otro verbo regular o irregular, empléense *DID* y *DID* NOT en la misma posición y orden en que aparecen con *to write*, utilizando en ambos el verbo principal en su forma simple.

Emplee únicamente el verbo principal en su forma de pasado en el afirmativo.

AUXILIARES PARA FORMAR EL FUTURO Y CONDICIONAL

Futuro	Condicional
Afirmativo	Afirmativo
WILL	WOULD
Negativo	Negativo
WILL NOT	WOULD NOT

Observe el empleo de *WILL* y *WOULD* antes de un verbo en su forma simple *(write)* para formar el *futuro* y *condicional.*

1. I	WILL	write many letters tomorrow
2. He	WILL	write many letters tomorrow
3. I	WOULD	write many letters now
4. He	WOULD	write many letters now

TRADUCCIÓN

1. Yo escribiré muchas cartas mañana
2. Él escribirá muchas cartas mañana
3. Yo escribiría muchas cartas ahora
4. Él escribiría muchas cartas ahora

NOTA: Empléanse *WILL* y *WOULD* con todos los pronombres: *I, you, he, she, it, we, you, they* en el inglés informal de uso cotidiano. *SHALL* y *SHOULD* se usan sólo en el inglés muy literario tal como la poesía o liturgia, pero únicamente en los pronombres *I* y *we.*

Observe la palabra NOT inmediatamente después de *WILL* y *WOULD* para formar el negativo del futuro y condicional.

1. I *will*	NOT	*write* many letters *tomorrow*
2. He *will*	NOT	*write* many letters *tomorrow*
3. I *would*	NOT	*write* many letters *now*
4. He *would*	NOT	*write* many letters *now*

TRADUCCIÓN

1. Yo no escribiré muchas cartas mañana
2. Él no escribirá muchas cartas mañana
3. Yo no escribiría muchas cartas hoy
4. Él no escribiría muchas cartas hoy

Nótese ahora que los auxiliares *WILL* y *WOULD* se anteponen a los pronombres *I, he*, etc., para formar preguntas.

1. **WILL**	I	*write* many letters *tomorrow?*
2. **WILL**	he	*write* many letters *tomorrow?*
3. **WOULD**	I	*write* many letters *now?*
4. **WOULD**	he	*write* many letters *now?*

TRADUCCIÓN

1. ¿Escribiré muchas cartas mañana?
2. ¿Escribirá él muchas cartas mañana?
3. ¿Escribiría yo muchas cartas ahora?
4. ¿Escribiría él muchas cartas ahora?

EL AUXILIAR *SHALL* EN SU USO MAS COMÚN

Observe en estas preguntas el uso práctico de *shall* con los pronombres *I* y *we* solamente para expresar *excitativa, invitación* o *iniciativa*. Note también que en esos casos *shall* expresa más bien una idea presente que futura.

SHALL	I *write*	that letter *now?*
SHALL	I *cut*	the cake *now?*
SHALL	we *dance?*	
SHALL	we *go?*	

TRADUCCIÓN

¿Escribo esa carta ahora?
¿Parto el pastel ahora?

¿Bailamos?
¿Nos vamos?

AUXILIARES QUE EXPRESAN *HABILIDAD, PERMISO* O *POSIBILIDAD*

HABILIDAD	POSIBILIDAD
Presente	Presente
CAN (puede)	MAY (posiblemente)
Pasado	Condicional o Pasado
COULD (pudo, podía)	MIGHT (podría)

Observe el verbo principal en su forma simple *(write)* después de los auxiliares *can, could, may* y *might*.

1. I	CAN	*write* many letters *daily*	
2. He	COULD	*write* many letters *yesterday*	
3. I	MAY	*write* a letter	*afterwards*
4. He	MIGHT	*write* a letter	*now*

TRADUCCIÓN

1. Yo puedo escribir muchas cartas diariamente
2. Él pudo escribir muchas cartas ayer

3. Posiblemente yo escriba una carta después
4. Él podría escribir una carta ahora

NOTA: Empléanse *can, could, may* y *might* con todos los pronombres o sujetos.

16

Nótese ahora que los auxiliares *can, could, may* y *might* se anteponen a los pronombres *I, he,* etc., para formar el interrogativo.

1. *CAN*	I *write* many letters *daily?*
2. *COULD*	he *write* many letters *yesterday?*
3. *MAY*	I *write* a letter *afterwards?*
4. *MIGHT*	he *write* a letter *now?*

TRADUCCIÓN

1. ¿Puedo escribir muchas cartas diariamente?
2. ¿Pudo él escribir muchas cartas ayer?
3. ¿Puedo escribir una carta después? (pidiendo permiso)
4. ¿Podría él escribir una carta ahora?

Observe la palabra NOT inmediatamente después de los auxiliares *can, could, may* y *might* para formar las negaciones.

1. I *can*	NOT	*write* many letters *daily*	
2. He *could*	NOT	*write* many letters *yesterday*	
3. I *may*	NOT	*write* a letter	*afterwards*
4. He *might*	NOT	*write* a letter	*now*

TRADUCCIÓN

1. Yo no puedo escribir muchas cartas diariamente.
2. Él no pudo escribir muchas cartas ayer
3. Posiblemente yo no escriba una carta después
4. Él podría no escribir una carta ahora

EL AUXILIAR *MAY* Y SUS TRES SIGNIFICADOS

MAY $\begin{cases} \text{Expresa:} \\ \text{1. } PERMISO \\ \text{2. } POSIBILIDAD \\ \text{3. } DESEO \end{cases}$

1. (Permiso) *MAY* I *write* a letter? (¿Puedo escribir una carta?)

2. (Posibilidad) I *MAY* write a letter. (Posiblemente yo escriba una carta.)

3. (Deseo) *MAY* you *write* a lovely poem! (¡Que escribas un hermoso poema!)

EL AUXILIAR *MIGHT* Y SUS DOS SIGNIFICADOS

MIGHT $\begin{cases} \text{Expresa:} \\ \text{1. } LIGERA\ POSIBILIDAD\ EN\ EL\ FUTURO \\ \text{2. } PERMISO\ EN\ PASADO \text{ (Forma en pasado} \\ \qquad\qquad\qquad\qquad\qquad \text{de } may) \end{cases}$

1. He says that he *might write* a book next year.
(Él dice que el podría escribir un libro el año próximo.)

2. Helen's mother said that she *might write* a letter to her boy-friend.
(La madre de Elena dijo que ella podía escribir una carta a su novio.)

18

LOS TRES AUXILIARES QUE EXPRESAN OBLIGACIÓN

EL TRIÁNGULO DEL DEBER

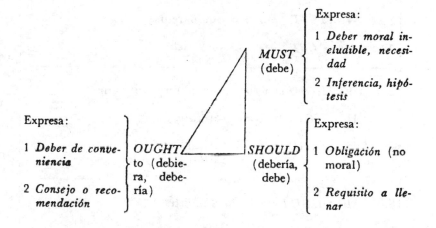

Expresa:

1 *Deber de conveniencia*

2 *Consejo o recomendación*

OUGHT to (debiera, debería)

SHOULD (debería, debe)

MUST (debe)

Expresa:

1 *Deber moral ineludible, necesidad*

2 *Inferencia, hipótesis*

Expresa:

1 *Obligación (no moral)*

2 *Requisito a llenar*

EJEMPLOS ILUSTRATIVOS

You *must* defend your country (Debes defender a tu país)
It *must* be very expensive (Debe ser muy caro)

They *should* follow instructions (Ellos deben seguir instrucciones)
I *should* bring my birth certificate (Debo traer mi acta de nacimiento)

You *ought to* know those things (Debes saber esas cosas)
He *ought to* rent that house (Él debe rentar esa casa)

Observe la carencia de *to* después de *must* y *should*, notando asimismo que estos dos auxiliares van seguidos de un verbo en su forma simple *(write, respect, honor, etc.)*. El auxiliar *ought* siempre va seguido de la partícula *to*.

1.	I *MUST* *write*	a letter	to my parentes *now*	
2.	You *MUST* *respect*	the law		
3.	We *MUST* *honor*	our parents		
4.	He *MUST* *be*	very rich		

5.	You *SHOULD* *write*	that letter	with ink	
6.	He *SHOULD* *drive*	carefully		
7.	They *SHOULD* *show*	their identification		

8.	He *OUGHT* *to* *learn* English
9.	You *OUGHT* *to* *see* a doctor

TRADUCCIÓN

1. Yo debo escribir una carta a mis padres ahora
2. Tú debes respetar la ley
3. Debemos honrar a nuestros padres
4. Él debe ser muy rico (suposición)

5. Deberías escribir esa carta con tinta
6. Él debería manejar con cuidado
7. Ellos deben mostrar su identificación

8. Él debiera (o debería) aprender inglés
9. Deberías o (debieras) ver a un médico

NOTA: Empléanse *MUST, SHOULD* y *OUGHT (to)* con todos los pronombres o sujetos.

Observe la palabra NOT inmediatamente después de los auxiliares *must, should* y *ought* para formar las negaciones. Nótese también la partícula *to* después de NOT en *ought*.

I *must*	NOT	*write* a letter	to my parents *now*
You *should*	NOT	*write* that letter	with ink
He *ought*	NOT	*to write* a letter	in Spanish

Ahora observe que los auxiliares *must, should* y *ought* (to) se anteponen a los pronombres *I, you, he*, etc., para formar el interrogativo. Nótese la partícula *to* antes de *write* en *ought*.

MUST	I	*write* a letter to my parents *now?*
SHOULD	you	*write* that letter with ink?
OUGHT	he	*to write* a letter in Spanish?

AUXILIAR *USED TO* PARA FORMAR EL PRETÉRITO IMPERFECTO (Historical Past)

PRETÉRITO IMPERFECTO

USED TO	Equivalente en castellano a las terminaciones del pasado, *ía, íamos, ían* o *aba, ábamos, aban*

Observe el verbo en infinitivo después de *USED (to write)*, así como su empleo en todos los sujetos o pronombres.

I	*USED*	*to* write	long letters	*many years ago*
He	*USED*	*to* read	good books	*many years ago*
We	*USED*	*to* speak	good English	*many years ago*
They	*USED*	*to* work	in Chicago	*many years ago*

TRADUCCIÓN

Yo escrib*ía* largas cartas hace muchos años

Él le*ía* buenos libros hace muchos años

Nosotros habl*ábamos* buen inglés hace muchos años

Ellos trabaj*aban* en Chicago hace muchos años

Observe el uso del DID NOT antes de *USE* para formar las negaciones. Nótese asimismo que la *d* de *used* desaparece en esta forma negativa.

I	DID NOT	*use to* write long letters *many years ago*
He	DID NOT	*use to* read good books *many years ago*
They	DID NOT	*use to* work in Chicago *many years ago*

Ahora observe el empleo de *DID* antes de los pronombres *I, he, they*, etc., para formar el interrogativo. También note la palabra *USE* en lugar de *used*.

DID	I	*use to* write	long letters *many years ago?*
DID	he	*use to* read	good books *many years ago?*
DID	they	*use to* work	in Chicago *many years ago?*

AUXILIARES QUE FORMAN EL ANTEPRESENTE Y ANTECOPRETÉRITO

Auxiliar del *Antepresente*		Auxiliar del *Antecopretérito*	
HAVE	he, has, ha, hemos, has. Empléase para: *I, you, we, you* y *they*	HAD	había, habías, habíamos, habían. Empléase para: *I, you, we, you* y *they*
HAS	Ha. Empléase para: *he, she, it*	HAD*	Había. Empléase para: *he, she, it*

* Como se puede ver, *had* se emplea con todos los pronombres personales o sujetos.

Observe la forma verbal en participio pasado *(written)* después de *HAVE, HAS* y *HAD*. No emplee *to* después de estos auxiliares para formar el *antepresente* y *antecopretérito*.

I	HAVE	*written* many letters *lately*
He	HAS	*written* many letters *lately*
They	HAVE	*written* many letters *lately*
I	HAD	*written* many letters *before*
He	HAD	*written* many letters *before*
They	HAD	*written* many letters *before*

TRADUCCIÓN

Yo he escrito muchas cartas últimamente
Él ha escrito muchas cartas últimamente
Ellos han escrito muchas cartas últimamente
Yo había escrito muchas cartas anteriormente
Él había escrito muchas cartas anteriormente
Ellos habían escrito muchas cartas anteriormente

NOTA: Cuando *have, has* y *had* van seguidos de la partícula *to*, entonces éstos expresan *necesidad, tener que*. Ejemplos:

I *have to* write a letter now (Tengo que escribir una carta ahora)
He *has to* go to school today (Él tiene que ir a la escuela hoy)
I *had to* write a letter yesterday (Yo tuve que escribir una carta ayer)

24

Observe la palabra NOT después de los auxiliares *have*, *has* y *had* para formar las negaciones.

I *have*	NOT	*written* many letters *lately*
He *has*	NOT	*written* many letters *lately*
They *have*	NOT	*written* many letters *lately*
I *had*	NOT	*written* many letters *before*
He *had*	NOT	*written* many letters *before*
They *had*	NOT	*written* many letters *before*

Ahora observe que los auxiliares *have, has* y *had* se anteponen a los pronombres *I, he, we, they,* etc., para formar el interrogativo.

HAVE	I *written* many letters *lately?*
HAS	he *written* many letters *lately?*
HAVE	they *written* many letters *lately?*
HAD	I *written* many letters *before?*
HAD	he *written* many letters *before?*
HAD	they *written* many letters *before?*

LA FORMA *GOING TO* PARA CONSTRUIR EL *FUTURO IDIOMÁTICO* Y EL *PASADO PROGRESIVO*

Futuro Idiomático	Pasado Progresivo
1. Am 2. Is } GOING TO 3. Are (1. voy) (2. va) (3. van)	1. Was 2. Were } GOING TO (1. iba) (2. iban)

Observe el empleo de los auxiliares *am, is, are, was* y *were* antes de GOING TO para formar el *futuro idiomático* y el *pasado progresivo*.

Nótese también el verbo en *infinitivo* (to write: escribir).

1. I	am	GOING	*to* write a letter *tomorrow*
2. He	is	GOING	*to* write a letter *tomorrow*
3. They	are	GOING	*to* write a letter *tomorrow*
4. I	was	GOING	*to* write a letter *yesterday*
5. He	was	GOING	*to* write a letter *yesterday*
6. They	were	GOING	*to* write a letter *yesterday*

TRADUCCIÓN

1. Yo voy a escribir una carta mañana
2. Él va a escribir una carta mañana
3. Ellos van a escribir una carta mañana
4. Yo iba a escribir una carta ayer
5. Él iba a escribir una carta ayer
6. Ellos iban a escribir una carta ayer

Observe la palabra NOT inmediatamente después de *am*, *is*, *are*, *was* y *were* y antes de GOING TO para formar el negativo del *futuro idiomático* y el *pasado progresivo*.

I *am*	NOT	*going to* write a letter *tomorrow*
He *is*	NOT	*going to* write a letter *tomorrow*
They *are*	NOT	*going to* write a letter *tomorrow*
I *was*	NOT	*going to* write a letter *yesterday*
He *was*	NOT	*going to* write a letter *yesterday*
They *were*	NOT	*going to* write a letter *yesterday*

TRADUCCIÓN

Yo no voy a escribir una carta mañana
Él no va a escribir una carta mañana
Ellos no van a escribir una carta mañana
Yo no iba a escribir una carta ayer
Él no iba a escribir una carta ayer
Ellos no iban a escribir una carta ayer

Advierta ahora que los auxiliares *am, is, are, was* y *were* se anteponen a los pronombres *I, he, they*, etc., para formar el interrogativo del *futuro idiomático* y el *pasado progresivo*. Note asimismo que la posición de GOING TO es igual que la del afirmativo. Es decir, conserva el tercer lugar en las oraciones afirmativas e interrogativas.

AM	I	*going to* write a letter *tomorrow?*
IS	he	*going to* write a letter *tomorrow?*
ARE	they	*going to* write a letter *tomorrow?*
WAS	I	*going to* write a letter *yesterday?*
WAS	he	*going to* write a letter *yesterday?*
WERE	they	*going to* write a letter *yesterday?*

FORMA *TO BE ABLE* PARA EXPRESAR EL FUTURO DE *PODER: WILL BE ABLE*

Futuro del verbo PODER (can)

WILL BE ABLE ⎰ Empléase en todos los pronombres: *I, you, he, she, it, we, you, they* y equivale a: *podrá, podrás, podremos, podrán*

Observe la partícula *to* inmediatamente después de la forma *WILL BE ABLE*, es decir, el verbo que le siga a dicha forma siempre en *infinitivo (to write).*

I	*WILL BE ABLE*	*to* write in English *very soon*
He	*WILL BE ABLE*	*to* write in English *very soon*
They	*WILL BE ABLE*	*to* write in English *very soon*

TRADUCCIÓN

Yo *podré* escribir en inglés muy pronto
Él *podrá* escribir en inglés muy pronto
Ellos *podrán* escribir en inglés muy pronto

NOTA: La traducción literal de TO BE ABLE es *ser capaz*, por tanto, I *will* BE ABLE significa literalmente *seré capaz.*

El verbo *can* (poder) carece de forma futura, toda vez que es defectivo, constando únicamente del presente *(can)* y el pasado *(could).*

Advierta la palabra NOT inmediatamente después del auxiliar *will* y antes de BE ABLE para formar las negaciones.

I *will*	NOT	*be able to* write in English
He *will*	NOT	*be able to* write in English
They *will*	NOT	*be able to* write in English

Nótese ahora que el auxiliar *will* se antepone a los pronombres *I, he, they,* etc., para formar el interrogativo. Observe también que la posición de las palabras *BE ABLE* es igual que la del afirmativo, o sea que ocupan el tercer lugar en las oraciones. En este caso después de los pronombres.

WILL	I	*be able to* write in English *soon?*
WILL	he	*be able to* write in English *soon?*
WILL	they	*be able to* write in English *soon?*

TRADUCCIÓN

¿Podré escribir en inglés pronto?

¿Podrá él escribir en inglés pronto?

¿Podrán ellos escribir en inglés pronto?

LOS AUXILIARES CON EL VERBO *HAVE* (haber) ESTRUCTURANDO LAS FORMAS COMPUESTAS

Will	HAVE *written*	= habrá escrito
Would	HAVE *written*	= habría escrito
Could	HAVE *written*	= pudo haber escrito
May	HAVE *written*	= posiblemente haya escrito
Might	HAVE *written*	= podría haber escrito
Must	HAVE *written*	= debe haber escrito
Should	HAVE *written*	= debería haber escrito
Ought	*to* HAVE *written*	= debiera haber escrito

Observe el empleo de *HAVE* después de todos los auxiliares. Nótese la partícula *to* después de *ought*, así como el verbo en participio *(written:* escrito) después de HAVE.

He *will*	HAVE	*written* a letter
He *would*	HAVE	*written* a letter
He *could*	HAVE	*written* a letter
He *may*	HAVE	*written* a letter
He *might*	HAVE	*written* a letter
He *must*	HAVE	*written* a letter
He *should*	HAVE	*written* a letter
He *ought*	*to* HAVE	*written* a letter

Observe la palabra NOT después de los auxiliares *will, would, could,* etc., para formar las negaciones. Nótese también que HAVE, que equivale al verbo haber, es invariable.

He *will*	NOT	have *written* a letter
He *would*	NOT	have *written* a letter
He *could*	NOT	have *written* a letter
He *may*	NOT	have *written* a letter
He *might*	NOT	have *written* a letter
He *must*	NOT	have *written* a letter
He *should*	NOT	have *written* a letter
He *ought*	NOT	*to* have *written* a letter

Observe ahora que los auxiliares *will, would, could,* etc., se anteponen al pronombre *he* para formar el interrogativo.

Nótese asimismo que la posición de HAVE no ha variado si se compara con la del afirmativo. Es decir, conserva su tercer lugar.

WILL	he	*have written* a letter?
WOULD	he	*have written* a letter?
COULD	he	*have written* a letter?
MAY	he	*have written* a letter?
MIGHT	he	*have written* a letter?
MUST	he	*have written* a letter?
SHOULD	he	*have written* a letter?
OUGHT	he *to*	*have written* a letter?

PRIMER GRUPO

VERBOS CON FORMAS IDÉNTICAS EN EL PASADO Y PARTICIPIO PASADO PERO CON INFINITIVO DISTINTO

Clasificación: *OUGHT*

Características: Terminación *OUGHT* (ot) para pasado y participio pasado, cuya pronunciación es *ot*. (*Bought* pronúnciese b*ot*).

Infinitivo	Pasado	Participio Pasado
1. *to* buy (comprar)	b*OUGHT* (compró)	b*OUGHT* (comprado)
2. *to* bring (traer)	br*OUGHT* (trajo)	br*OUGHT* (traído)
3. *to* think (pensar o creer)	th*OUGHT* (pensó o creyó)	th*OUGHT* (pensado o creído)
4. *to* seek (buscar)	s*OUGHT* (buscó)	s*OUGHT* (buscado)
5. *to* fight (pelear, combatir)	f*OUGHT* (peleó, combatió)	f*OUGHT* (peleado, combatido)

Ejemplos ilustrativos de cómo emplear el verbo marcado con el número 1 en sus tiempos y formas fundamentales: clasificación *OUGHT*

Infinitivo

John wants *to* buy a new automobile.
(Juan quiere comprar un automóvil nuevo.)

Presente

(af.) They buy many groceries *every Saturday.*
(Ellos compran muchos víveres todos los sábados.)

(neg.) They DO NOT buy many groceries *every Saturday.*

(int.) DO they buy many groceries *every Saturday?*

Pasado

(af.) They b*OUGHT* many groceries *last Saturday.*
(Ellos compraron muchos víveres el sábado pasado.)

(neg.) They DID NOT *buy* many groceries *last Saturday.*

(int.) DID they *buy* many groceries *last Saturday?*

Antepresente

(af.) They *have* b*OUGHT* many clothes during this month.
(Ellos han comprado mucha ropa durante este mes.)

(neg.) They *have* NOT b*OUGHT* many clothes during this month.

(int.) *Have* they b*OUGHT* many clothes this month?

Ejemplos ilustrativos de cómo emplear el verbo marcado con el número 2 en sus tiempos y formas fundamentales: clasificación *OUGHT*.

Infinitivo

I expect *to* bring my camera to school.
(Espero traer mi cámara a la escuela.)

Presente

(af.) We bring presents for the family *every Christmas.*
(Traemos regalos para la familia cada Navidad.)

(neg.) We DO NOT bring presents for the family *every Christmas.*

(int.) DO we bring presents for the family *every Christmas?*

Pasado

(af.) We br*OUGHT* presents for the family *last Christmas.*
(Trajimos regalos para la familia la Navidad pasada.)

(neg.) We DID NOT *bring* presents for the family *last Christmas.*

(int.) DID we *bring* presents for the family *last Christmas?*

(af.) He *has* br*OUGHT* the packages from the store.
(Él ha traído los paquetes de la tienda.)

(neg.) He *has* NOT br*OUGHT* the packages from the store.

(int.) *Has* he br*OUGHT* the packages from the store?

Ejemplos ilustrativos de cómo emplear el verbo marcado con el número 3 en sus tiempos y formas fundamentales: clasificación *OUGHT*.

Infinitivo

I need *to* think about this matter carefully.
(Necesito pensar en este asunto cuidadosamente.)

Presente

(af.) He think*s* *of* his family *every day*.
(Él piensa en su familia todos los días.)

(neg.) He DOES NOT think *of* his family *every day*.

(int.) DOES he think *of* his family *every day?*

Pasado

(af.) He th*OUGHT* *of* his family when he was away.
(Él pensó en su familia cuando estuvo fuera.)

(neg.) He DID NOT *think of* his family when he was away.

(int.) DID he *think of* his family when he was away?

Antepresente

(af.) You *have* th*OUGHT* *of* him very much lately.
(Usted ha pensado mucho en él últimamente.)

(neg.) You *have* NOT th*OUGHT* *of* him very much lately.

(int.) *Have* you th*OUGHT* *of* him very much lately?

Ejemplos ilustrativos de cómo emplear el verbo marcado con el número 4 en sus tiempos y formas fundamentales: clasificación *OUGHT*.

Infinitivo

I intend *to* seek for another position next month.
(Tengo intenciones de buscar otra colocación el mes próximo.)

Presente

(af.) He seeks a good position.
(Él busca una buena colocación.)

(neg.) He DOES NOT seek a good position.

(int.) DOES he *seek* a good position?

Pasado

(af.) George s*OUGHT* for an apartment *last year*.
(Jorge buscó un departamento el año pasado.)

(neg.) George DID NOT *seek* for an apartment *last year*.

(int.) DID George *seek* for an apartment *last year?*

Antepresente

(af.) My uncle *has* s*OUGHT* for legal advice.
(Mi tío ha buscado consejo legal.)

(neg.) My uncle *has* NOT s*OUGHT* for legal advice.

(int.) *Has* my uncle s*OUGHT* for legal advice?

Ejemplos ilustrativos de cómo emplear el verbo marcado con el número 5 en sus tiempos y formas fundamentales: clasificación *OUGHT*.

Infinitivo

Richard *does not* like *to* fight with their friends.
(A Ricardo no le gusta pelear con sus amigos.)

Presente

(af.) John and Charles fight *every day*.
(Juan y Carlos se pelean todos los días.)

(neg.) John and Charles DO NOT fight *every day*.

(int.) DO John and Charles fight *every day?*

Pasado

(af.) My grandfather f*OUGHT* in the Civil War.
(Mi abuelo combatió en la guerra civil.)

(neg.) My grandfather DID NOT *fight* in the Civil War.

(int.) DID my granfather *fight* in the Civil War?

Antepresente

(af.)   Those gangsters *have* f*OUGHT* among themselves.
(Esos hampones se han peleado entre ellos mismos.)

(neg.) Those gangsters *have* NOT f*OUGHT* among themselves.

(int.)   *Have* those gangsters f*OUGHT* among themselves?

Sub-clasificación: *AUGHT* (pronúnciese igual que *ought:* ot)

Infinitivo	Pasado	Participio Pasado
1. *to* teach (enseñar)	t*AUGHT* (enseñó)	t*AUGHT* (enseñado)
2. *to* catch (coger, atrapar)	c*AUGHT* (cogió, atrapó)	c*AUGHT* (cogido, atrapado)

Ejemplos ilustrativos de cómo emplear el verbo marcado con el número 1 en sus tiempos y formas fundamentales: clasificación *AUGHT*.

Infinitivo

He plans *to* teach Anatomy in the university.
(Él proyecta enseñar Anatomía en la universidad.)

Presente

(af.)   You teach Arithmetic *every day*.
(Usted enseña aritmética todos los días.)

(neg.) You DO NOT *teach* Arithmetic *every day*.

(int.)   DO you *teach* Arithmetic *every day?*

Pasado

(af.)   She t*AUGHT* English *last year*.
(Ella enseñó inglés el año pasado.)

(neg.) She DID NOT *teach* English *last year*.

(int.)   DID she *teach* English *last year?*

Antepresente

(af.) She *has* t*AUGHT* them to speak Spanish.
(Ella les ha enseñado a hablar español.)

(neg.) She *has* NOT t*AUGHT* them to speak Spanish.

(int.) *Has* she t*AUGHT* them to speak Spanish?

Ejemplos ilustrativos de cómo emplear el verbo marcado con el número 2 en sus tiempos y formas fundamentales: clasificación *AUGHT*.

Infinitivo

He wants *to* catch the bus on time.
(Él quiere tomar [coger] el autobús a tiempo.)

Presente

(af.) You catch this bus *every day*.
(Usted toma [coge] este autobús todos los días.)

(neg.) You DO NOT *catch* this bus *every day*.

(int.) DO you *catch* this bus *every day?*

Pasado

(af.) Henry c*AUGHT* a cold *last week*.
(Enrique se resfrió [cogió un resfriado] la semana pasada.)

(neg.) Henry DID NOT *catch* a cold *last week*.

(int.) DID Henry *catch* a cold *last week?*

Antepresente

(af.) The policeman *has* c*AUGHT* the thief.
(El policía ha capturado [atrapado] al ladrón.)

(neg.) The policeman *has* NOT c*AUGHT* the thief.

(int.) *Has* the policeman c*AUGHT* the thief?

Clasificación: *EE* o *EA, E - T*.

Características: Los infinitivos de este grupo constan de dos vocales seguidas (to sl*ee*p, to l*ea*ve). En el pasado y participio pasado la segunda vocal desaparece y ambas formas terminan en *t* (slep*t*, lef*t*). En este caso la *ee* y la *ea* tienen un sonido equivalente a la *i* latina. En el pasado y participio pasado la *e* suena como en español.

Infinitivo	Pasado	Participio Pasado
1. *to* sl*EE*p (dormir)	sl*E*p*T* (durmió)	sl*E*p*T* (dormido)
2. *to* k*EE*p (guardar, conservar)	k*E*p*T* (guardó, conservó)	k*E*p*T* (guardado, conservado)
3. *to* sw*EE*p (barrer)	sw*E*p*T* (barrió)	sw*E*p*T* (barrido)
4. *to* w*EE*p (llorar,	w*E*p*T* (lloró,	w*E*p*T* (llorado,
5. *to* cr*EE*p arrastrarse, deslizarse)	cr*E*p*T* (se arrastró, se deslizó)	cr*E*p*T* (arrastrado, deslizado)

6. *to* f*EE*l (sentir)	f*E*l*T* (sintió)	f*E*l*T* (sentido)
7 *to* kn*EE*l (arrodillarse)	kn*E*l*T* (se arrodilló)	kn*E*l*T* (arrodillado)
8. *to* m*EE*t (encontrarse, conocerse)	m*E*T* (se encontró, conoció)	m*E*T* (encontrado, conocido)

9. *to* l*EA*ve (salir, dejar)	l*E*f*T* (salió, dejó)	l*E*f*T* (salido, dejado)
10. *to* ber*EA*ve (asolar, acongojar)	ber*E*f*T* (asoló, acongojó)	ber*E*f*T* (asolado, acongojado)

Ejemplos ilustrativos de cómo emplear el verbo marcado con el número 1 en sus tiempos y formas fundamentales: clasificación *EE* o *EA, E-T*

Infinitivo

Helen likes *to* sleep more than eight hours.
(A Elena le gusta dormir más de ocho horas.)

Presente

(af.)   Helen sleeps eight hours *every day*.
(Elena duerme ocho horas todos los días.)

(neg.)   Helen DOES NOT sleep eight hours *every day*

(int.)   DOES Helen sleep eight hours *every day?*

Pasado

(af.)   You slEpT very little *last night*.
(Tú dormiste muy poco anoche)

(neg.)   You DID NOT sleep very little *last night*.

(int.)   DID you sleep very little *last night?*

Antepresente

(af.)   They *have* slEpT here lately.
(Ellos han dormido aquí últimamente.)

(neg.)   They *have* NOT slEpT here lately.

(int.)   *Have* they slEpT here lately?

Ejemplos ilustrativos de cómo emplear el verbo marcado con el número 2 en sus tiempos y formas fundamentales: clasificación *EE* o *EA, E-T.*

Infinitivo

He does not want *to* keep his money *in* the Bank.
(Él no quiere guardar su dinero en el banco.)

Presente

(af.)   Mother keeps the bread hot in the oven *every day*.
(Mamá conserva el pan caliente en el horno todos los días.)

(neg.) Mother DOES NOT keep the bread hot in the oven *every day.*

(int.) DOES mother keep the bread hot in the oven *every day?*

Pasado

(af.) I kEpT the keys *in* my pocket.
(Guardé las llaves en mi bolsillo.)

(neg.) I DID NOT keep the keys *in* my pocket.

(int.) DID I keep the keys *in* my pocket?

Antepresente

(af.) The girl *has* kEpT the meat *in* the freezer.
(La muchacha ha guardado lá carne en el congelador.)

(neg.) The girl *has* NOT kEpT the meat *in* the freezer.

(int.) *Has* the girl kEpT the meat *in* the freezer?

Ejemplos ilustrativos de cómo emplear el verbo marcado con el número 3 en sus tiempos y formas fundamentales: clasificación *EE* o *EA, E-T*.

Infinitivo

The girl has *to* sweep the floor every day.
(La muchacha tiene que barrer el piso todos los días.)

Presente

(af.) The girl sweeps the floor *every day.*
(La muchacha barre el piso todos los días.)

(neg.) The girl DOES NOT sweep the floor *every day.*

(int.) DOES the girl sweep the floor *every day?*

Pasado

(af.) The girl swEpT the floor *yesterday.*
(La muchacha barrió el piso ayer.)

(neg.) The girl DID NOT sweep the floor *yesterday.*

(int.) DID the girl sweep the floor *yesterday?*

Antepresente

(af.) Mary *has* swEpT the floor every day this week.
(María ha barrido el piso todos los días esta semana.)

(neg.) Mary *has* NOT swEpT the floor every day this week.

(int.) *Has* Mary swEpT the floor every day this week?

Ejemplos ilustrativos de cómo emplear el verbo marcado con el número 4 en sus tiempos y formas fundamentales: clasificación *EE* o *EA, E-T*.

Infinitivo

She does not have *to* weep all the time.
(Ella no tiene que sollozar todo el tiempo.)

Presente

(af.) Women usually weep easily over trivial things.
(Las mujeres generalmente lloran fácilmente por cosas triviales.)

(neg.) Women DO NOT usually weep easily over trivial things.

(int.) DO women usually weep easily over trivial things?

Pasado

(af.) The woman wEpT very much after the accident.
(La mujer lloró mucho después del accidente.)

(neg.) The woman DID NOT weep very much after the accident.

(int.) DID the woman weep very much after the accident?

Antepresente

(af.) They *have* wEpT quietly during the funeral.
(Ellos han llorado calladamente durante el funeral.)

(neg.) They *have* NOT wEpT quietly during the funeral.

(int.) *Have* they wEpT quietly during the funeral?

Ejemplos ilustrativos de cómo emplear el verbo marcado con el número 5 en sus tiempos y formas fundamentales: clasificación *EE* o *EA, E-T*.

Infinitivo

You do not have *to* creep on the floor.
(Tú no tienes que arrastrarte en el piso.)

Presente

(af.) Tigers creep quietly in the darkness.
(Los tigres se deslizan calladamente en la oscuridad.)

(neg.) Tigers DO NOT creep quietly in the darkness.

(int.) DO tigers creep quietly in the darkness?

Pasado

(af.) The lava from the volcano cr*E*p*T* over the valley.
(La lava del volcán se deslizó sobre el valle.)

(neg.) The lava from the volcano DID NOT creep over the valley.

(int.) DID the lava from the volcano creep over the valley?

Antepresente

(af.) The little dog *has* cr*E*p*T* over the ground.
(El perrito se ha arrastrado por el suelo.)

(neg.) The little dog *has* NOT cr*E*p*T* over the ground.

(int.) *Has* the little dog cr*E*p*T* over the ground?

Ejemplos ilustrativos de cómo emplear el verbo marcado con el número 6 en sus tiempos y formas fundamentales: clasificación *EE* o *EA, E T*.

Infinitivo

She likes *to* feel sorry for herself.
(Le gusta compadecerse a sí misma [sentir pena de sí misma].)

Presente

(af.) My grandfather feels tired *every morning*.
(Mi abuelo se siente cansado todas las mañanas.)

(neg.)   My grandfather DOES NOT feel tired *every morning*.

(int.)   DOES my grandfather feel tired *every morning?*

Pasado

(af.)   The students fElT tired after the tour *yesterday*.
(Los estudiantes se sintieron cansados después de la excursión, ayer.)

(neg.)   The students DID NOT feel tired after the tour *yesterday*.

(int).   DID the students feel tired after the tour *yesterday?*

Antepresente

(af.)   You *have* fElT cold during the Winter.
(Usted ha sentido frío durante el invierno.)

(neg.)   You *have* NOT fElT cold during the Winter.

(int.)   *Have* you fElT cold during the Winter?

Ejemplos ilustrativos de cómo emplear el verbo marcado con el número 7 en sus tiempos y formas fundamentales: clasificación *EE* o *EA, E-T*.

Infinitivo

You have *to* kneel in church.
(Usted tiene que arrodillarse en la iglesia.)

Presente

(af.)   Mary kneels in church *every day*.
(María se arrodilla en la iglesia todos los días.)

(neg.)   Mary DOES NOT kneel in church *every day*.

(int.)   DOES Mary kneel in church *every day?*

Pasado

(af.)   Mary knElT in church *yesterday*.
(María se arrodilla en la iglesia todos los días.)

(neg.)   Mary DID NOT kneel in church *yesterday*.

(int.)   DID Mary kneel in church *yesterday?*

Antepresente

(af.)   Mary *has* kn*El*T in church during Mass.
(María se ha arrodillado en la iglesia durante la misa.)

(neg.) Mary *has* NOT kn*El*T in church during Mass.

(int.) *Has* Mary kn*El*T in church during Mass?

Ejemplos ilustrativos de cómo emplear el verbo marcado con el número 8 en sus tiempos y formas fundamentales: clasificación *EE* o *EA, E-T*.

Infinitivo

I would like *to* meet new friends.
(Me gustaría conecer nuevas amistades.)

Presente

(af.)   They meet many friends at the club *every day*.
(Ellos encuentran muchos amigos en el club todos los días.)

(neg.) They DO NOT meet many friends at the club *every day*.

(int.) DO they meet many friends at the club *every day?*

Pasado

(af.)   They m*ET* many friends at the club *yesterday*.
(Ellos se encontraron muchos amigos en el club ayer.)

(neg.) They DID NOT meet many friends at the club *yesterday*.

(int.) DID they meet many friends at the club *yesterday?*

Antepresente

(af.)   They *have* m*ET* many people in New York.
(Ellos han conocido a mucha gente en Nueva York.)

(neg.) They *have* NOT m*ET* many people in New York.

(int.) *Have* they m*ET* many people in New York?

44

Ejemplos ilustrativos de cómo emplear el verbo marcado con el número 9 en sus tiempos y formas fundamentales: clasificación *EE* o *EA, E-T.*

Infinitivo

John wants *to* leave early.
(Juan quiere salir temprano.)

Presente

(af.) He leaves the office at six o'clock *every day.*
(Él sale de la oficina a la seis todos los días.)

(neg.) He DOES NOT leave the office at six o'clock *every day.*

(int.) DOES he leave the office at six o'clock *every day?*

Pasado

(af.) He lEfT the office at six o'clock *yesterday.*
(El salió de la oficina a las seis ayer.)

(neg.) He DID NOT leave the office at six o'clock *yesterday.*

(int). DID he leave the office at six o'clock *yesterday?*

Antepresente

(af.) Mr. Smith *has* lEfT the books on the table.
(El señor Smith ha dejado los libros sobre la mesa.)

(neg.) Mr. Smith *has* NOT lEfT the books on the table.

(int.) *Has* Mr. Smith lEfT the books on the table?

Ejemplos ilustrativos de cómo emplear el verbo marcado con el número 10 en sus tiempos y formas fundamentales: clasificación *EE* o *EA, E-T.*

Infinitivo

He does not want *to* bereave his family.
(Él no quiere acongojar a su familia.)

Presente

(af.) Henry bereaves his mother *every day.*
(Enrique acongoja a su madre todos los días.)

(neg.) Henry DOES NOT ber*e*ave his mother *every day*.
(int.) DOES Henry ber*e*ave his mother *every day?*

Pasado

(af.) Henry ber*Eſ*T his mother *yesterday*.
(Enrique acongojó a su madre ayer.)
(neg.) Henry DID NOT ber*e*ave his mother *yesterday*.
(int.) DID Henry ber*e*ave his mother *yesterday?*

Antepresente

(af.) The hurricane *has* ber*Eſ*T the valley.
(El ciclón ha asolado al valle.)
(neg.) The hurricane *has* not ber*Eſ*T the valley.
(int.) *Has* the hurricane ber*Eſ*T the valley?

Clasificación: *EE* o *EA, E-T.*

Características: Tanto el infinitivo como el pasado y participio pasado de esta clasificación poseen la combinación de las vocales *ea* (excepto *to dwell).* El pasado y participio pasado de estos verbos irregulares se forma añadiendo una *t* a cada uno de sus infinitivos. La combinación *ea* tiene sonido de *i* latina en el infinitivo y en el pasado y participio pasado de *e* castellana.

Infinitivo	Pasado	Participio Pasado
1. *to* deal (tratar, comerciar)	d*EA*lT (trató, comerció)	d*EA*lT (tratado, comerciado)
2. to m*EA*n (significar, querer decir)	m*EA*nT (significó, quiso decir)	m*EA*nT (significado, querido decir)
3. *to* leap (saltar)	l*EA*pT (saltó)	l*EA*pT (saltado)
4. *to* dwell (habitar)	dw*E*lT (habitó)	dw*E*lT (habitado)

Ejemplos ilustrativos de cómo emplear el verbo marcado con el número 1 en sus tiempos y formas fundamentales: clasificación *EA, EA-T.*

Infinitivo

I do not like *to* deal with those people.
(No me gusta comerciar con esa gente.)

Presente

(af.)   They deal with many buyers *every day.*
       (Ellos tratan con muchos compradores todos los días.)

(neg.) They DO NOT deal with many buyers *every day.*

(int.) DO they deal with many buyers *every day?*

Pasado

(af.)   They d*EA*1T with many buyers *last year*.
        (Ellos trataron con muchos compradores el año pasado.)

(neg.)   They DID NOT deal with many buyers *last year*.

(int.)   DID they deal with many buyers *last year?*

Antepresente

(af.)   Mr. Brown *has* d*EA*1T with foreign importers.
        (El señor Brown ha comerciado con importadores extranjeros.)

(neg.)   Mr. Brown *has* NOT d*EA*1T with foreign importers.

(int.)   *Has* Mr. Brown d*EA*1T with foreign importers?

Ejemplos ilustrativos de cómo emplear el verbo marcado con el número 2 en sus tiempos y formas fundamentales: clasificación *EA*, *EA-T*.

Infinitivo

Monkeys like *to* leap from one tree-branch to another.
(A los monos les gusta saltar de una rama de un **árbol** a otra)

Presente

(af.)   That monkey leaps inside his cage *every day*.
        (Ese mono salta dentro de su jaula todos los días.)

(neg.)   That monkey DOES NOT leap inside his cage *every day*.

(int.)   DOES that monkey leap inside his cage *every day?*

Pasado

(af.)   That monkey *lEApT* inside his cage *yesterday*.
        (Ese mono saltó dentro de su jaula ayer.)

(neg.)   That monkey DID NOT leap inside his cage *yesterday*.

(int.)   DID that monkey leap inside his cage *yesterday?*

Antepresente

(af.)   The walrus *have* *lEApT* during the circus show.
        (Las morsas han saltado durante la función de circo.)

(neg.) The walrus *have* NOT lEApT during the circus show.

(int.) *Have* the walrus lEApT during the circus show?

Ejemplos ilustrativos de cómo emplear el verbo marcado con el número 4 en sus tiempos y formas fundamentales: clasificación *EA, EA-T*.

Infinitivo

My parents would like *to* dwell in a bigger house.
(A mis padres les gustaría habitar una casa más grande.)

Presente

(af.) Some primitive tribes dwell in huts.
(Algunas tribus no civilizadas habitan en chozas.)

(neg.) Some primitive tribes DO NOT dwell in huts.

(int.) DO some primitive tribes dwell in huts?

Pasado

(af.) The cave-man dwElT in caves many years *ago*.
(El hombre cavernario habitó en cuevas hace muchos años.)

(neg.) The cave-man DID NOT dwell in caves many years *ago*.

(int.) DID the cave-man dwell in caves many years *ago*?

Antepresente

(af.) Civilized people *have* dwElT in houses for many years.
(La gente civilizada ha habitado en casas por muchos años.)

(neg.) Civilized people *have* NOT dwElT in houses for many years.

(int.) *Have* civilized people dwElT in houses for many years?

Clasificación: *EE* o *EA, ED.*

Características: En este grupo los infinitivos constan de dos vocales seguidas (to f*ee*d, to l*ea*d) cuyo sonido equivale a la *i* latina. En el pasado y participio pasado se elimina una de las vocales quedando siempre la vocal *e*, conservando el mismo sonido que tiene en castellano.

Nótese que las tres formas terminan en *d*, excepto el infinitivo de *to flee* (huir).

	Infinitivo	Pasado	Participio Pasado
1.	*to* feed (dar de comer, alimentar)	f*ED* (dio de comer, alimentó)	f*ED* (dado de comer, alimentado)
2.	*to* speed (acelerar)	sp*ED* (aceleró)	sp*ED* (acelerado)
3.	*to* bleed (sangrar)	bl*ED* (sangró)	bl*ED* (sangrado)
4.	*to* breed (criar, procrear)	br*ED* (crió, procreó)	br*ED* (criado, procreado)
5.	*to* lead (conducir, guiar)	l*ED* (condujo, guió, dirigió)	l*ED* (conducido, guiado, dirigido)
6.	*to* flee (huir)	fl*ED* (huyó)	fl*ED* (huido)

Sub-clasificación: *EA, EAD.*

Características: Obsérvese que las vocales *ea* son comunes en el infinitivo, en tanto que *ead* lo son el el pasado y participio pasado. *EA* tiene sonido de *i* latina en el infinitivo y en el pasado y participio pasado estas mismas vocales juntas tienen sonido de *e* castellana.

	Infinitivo	Pasado	Participio Pasado
1.	*to* read (leer)	r*EAD* (leyó)	r*EAD* (leído)
2.	*to* hear (oir)	h*EA*r*D* (oyó)	h*EA*r*D* (oído)

Ejemplos ilustrativos de cómo emplear el verbo marcado con el número 1 en sus tiempos y formas fundamentales: clasificación *EE* o *EA, ED*.

Infinitivo

The little girl likes *to* feed the chicken.
(A la muchachita le gusta dar de comer a los pollos.)

Presente

(af.)   She feeds the children *every day*.
(Ella da de comer a los niños todos los días.)

(neg.)   She DOES NOT feed the children *every day*.

(int.)   DOES she feed the children *every day?*

Pasado

(af.)   She f*ED* the children *yesterday*.
(Ella dio de comer a los niños ayer.)

(neg.)   She DID NOT feed the children *yesterday*.

(int.)   DID she feed the children *yesterday?*

Antepresente

(af.)   They *have* f*ED* themselves with milk and vegetables.
(Ellos se han alimentado con leche y verduras.)

(neg.)   They *have* NOT f*ED* themselves with milk and vegetables.

(int.)   *Have* they f*ED* themselves with milk and vegetables?

Ejemplos ilustrativos de cómo emplear el verbo marcado con el número 2 en sus tiempos y formas fundamentales: clasificación *EE* o *EA, ED*.

Infinitivo

John likes *to* speed his car on the highway.
(A Juan le gusta acelerar su auto en la carretera.)

Presente

(af.)   He speeds his motorcycle on the free-way.
(Él acelera su motocicleta en el viaducto.)

(neg.) He DOES NOT speed his motorcycle on the free-way.

(int.) DOES he speed his motorcycle on the free-way?

Pasado

(af.) He spED his motorcycle on the free-way *yesterday*.
(Él aceleró su motocicleta en el viaducto ayer.)

(neg.) He DID NOT speed his motorcycle on the free-way *yesterday*.

(int.) DID he speed his motorcycle on the free-way *yesterday?*

Antepresente

(af.) John *has* spED his car on the highway.
(Juan ha acelerado su auto en la carretera.)

(neg.) John *has* NOT spED his car on the highway.

(int.) *Has* John spED his car on the highway?

Ejemplos ilustrativos de cómo emplear el verbo marcado con el número 3 en sus tiempos y formas fundamentales: clasificación *EE* o *EA, ED*.

Infinitivo

The wound does not have *to* bleed after de operation.
(La herida no tiene que sangrar después de la operación.)

Presente

(af.) Robert bleeds through his nose because of the hot weather.
(Roberto sangra por la nariz debido al tiempo caluroso.)

(neg.) Robert DOES NOT bleed through his nose because of the hot weather.

(int.) DOES Robert bleed through his nose because of the hot weather?

Pasado

(af.) Robert blED through his nose because of the hot weather.
(Roberto sangró por la nariz debido al tiempo caluroso.)

(neg.) Robert DID NOT bl*ee*d through his nose because of the hot weather.

(int.) DID Robert bleed through his nose because of the hot weather?

Antepresente

(af.) He *has* bl*ED* through his wound after the operation.
(Él ha sangrado por su herida después de la operación.)

(neg.) He *has* NOT bl*ED* through his wound after the operation.

(int.) *Has* he bl*ED* through his wound after the operation?

Ejemplos ilustrativos de cómo emplear el verbo marcado con el número 4 en sus tiempos y formas fundamentales: clasificación *EE* o *EA, ED.*

Infinitivo

My uncle plans *to* breed race horses.
(Mi tío proyecta criar caballos de carreras.)

Presente

(af.) They br*ee*d cattle on their ranch.
(Ellos crian ganado en su rancho.)

(neg.) They DO NOT breed cattle on their ranch.

(int.) DO they breed cattle on their ranch?

Pasado

(af.) They br*ED* cattle on their ranche *last year.*
(Ellos criaron ganado en su rancho el año pasado.)

(neg.) They DID NOT breed cattle on their ranch *last year.*

(int.) DID they breed cattle on their ranch *last year?*

Antepresente

(af.) They *have* br*ED* cattle *for many years.*
(Ellos han criado ganado por muchos años.)

(neg.) They *have* NOT br*ED* cattle *for many years.*

(int.) *Have* they br*ED* cattle *for many years?*

Ejemplos ilustrativos de cómo emplear el verbo marcado con el número 5 en sus tiempos y formas fundamentales: clasificación *EE* o *EA, ED*.

Infinitivo

He likes *to* lead people through the museum.
(A él le gusta guiar a la gente por el museo.)

Presente

(af.)   My cousin leads tourists through the city.
(Mi primo guía a los turistas por la ciudad.)

(neg.)   My cousin DOES NOT lead tourists through the city.

(int.)   DOES my cousin lead tourists through the city?

Pasado

(af.)   My cousin lED some tourists through the city *yesterday*.
(Mi primo guió a unos turistas por la ciudad ayer.)

(neg.)   My cousin DID NOT lead some tourists through the city *yesterday*.

(int.)   DID my cousin lead some tourists through the city *yesterday?*

Antepresente

(af.)   He *has* lED many tourists to the station.
(Él ha conducido a muchos turistas a la estación.)

(neg.)   He *has* NOT lED many tourists to the station.

(int.)   *Has* he lED many tourists to the station?

Ejemplos ilustrativos de cómo emplear el verbo marcado con el número 6 en sus tiempos y formas fundamentales: clasificación *EE* o *EA, ED*.

Infinitivo

They tried *to* flee to a free country.
(Ellos trataron de huir a un país libre.)

Presente

(af.) Some birds fl*ee* to warmer climates *every year.*
(Algunas aves huyen a climas más cálidos todos los años.)

(neg.) Some birds DO NOT fl*ee* to warmer climates every year.

(int.) DO some birds fl*ee* to warmer climates *every year?*

Pasado

(af.) Some birds fl*ED* to warmer climates *last year.*
(Algunas aves huyeron a climas más cálidos el año pasado.)

(neg.) Some birds DID NOT fl*ee* to warmer climates *last year.*

(int.) DID some birds fl*ee* to warmer climates *last year?*

Antepresente

(af.) Some birds *have* fl*ED* to warmer lands during this Winter.
(Algunas aves han huido a tierras más cálidas durante este invierno.)

(neg.) Some birds *have* NOT fl*ED* to warmer lands during this Winter.

(int.) *Have* some birds fl*ED* to warmer lands during this Winter?

Ejemplos ilustrativos de cómo emplear el verbo marcado con el número 1 en sus tiempos y formas fundamentales: subclasificación *EA, EAD.*

Infinitivo

Mi brother likes *to* read scientific books.
(A mi hermano le gusta leer libros científicos.)

Presente

(af.) John reads the newspaper *every night.*
(Juan lee el periódico todas las noches.)

(neg.) John DOES NOT r*ead* the newspaper *every night.*

(int.) DOES John r*ead* the newspaper *last night?*

Pasado

(af.) John r*EAD* the newspaper *last night.*
(Juan leyó el periódico anoche.)

(neg.) John DID NOT read the newspaper *last night.*

(int.) DID John read the newspaper *last night?*

Antepresente

(af.) Dr. Jones *has* r*EAD* many books during his life.
(El doctor Jones ha leído muchos libros durante su vida.)

(neg.) Dr. Jones *has* NOT r*EAD* many books during his life.

(int.) *Has* Dr. Jones r*EAD* many books during his life?

Ejemplos ilustrativos de cómo emplear el verbo marcado con el número 2 en sus tiempos y formas fundamentales: sub-clasificación *EA, EAD.*

Infinitivo

The teacher does not like *to hear* noise in the classroom.
(Al maestro no le gusta oir ruido en el aula.)

Presente

(af.) They always h*ear* loud voices out in the street *every morning.*
(Ellos siempre oyen fuertes voces en la calle todas las mañanas.)

(neg.) They DO NOT always h*ear* loud voices in the street *every morning.*

(int.) DO they always h*ear* loud voices out in the street *every morning?*

Pasado

(af.) They h*EArD* loud voices out in the street *last night.*
(Ellos oyeron fuertes voces en la calle anoche.)

(neg.)   They DID NOT hear loud voices out in the street *last night.*

(int.)   DID they hear loud voices out in the street *last night?*

Antepresente

(af.)   The employees *have* hEArD good news about the sharing of the profits.
(Los empleados han oído buenas noticias acerca del reparto de utilidades.)

(neg.)   The employees *have* NOT.hEArD good news about the sharing of the profits.

(int.)   *Have* the employees hEArD good news about the sharing of the profits?

Clasificación. *D, T.*

Características: Todos sus infinitivos terminan en *d* (spen*d*), cuya consonante se cambia por *t* (spen*t*) para dar origen al pasado y participio pasado.

	Infinitivo	Pasado	Participio Pasado
1.	*to* spen*D** (gastar)	spen*T* (gastó)	spen*T* (gastado)
2.	*to* sen*D* (enviar)	sen*T* (envió)	sen*T* (enviado)
3.	*to* len*D* (prestar)	len*T* (prestó)	len*T* (prestado)
4.	*to* ben*D* (doblar, encorvar)	ben*T* (dobló, encorvó)	ben*T* (doblado, encorvado)
5.	*to* buil*D*** construir)	buil*T* (construyó)	buil*T* (construido)

* Empléase *to spend* en el sentido de gastar dinero o tiempo (pasar el tiempo cuando implica estancia, permanencia).
** La *u* de build, built, built, es muda.

Ejemplos ilustrativos de cómo emplear el verbo marcado con el número 1 en sus tiempos y formas fundamentales: clasificación *D, T.*

Infinitivo

I am going *to* spen*d* my vacation on the beach.
(Voy a pasar mis vacaciones en la playa.)

Presente

(af.) John spen*ds* too much money *every Sunday*.
(Juan gasta demasiado dinero los domingos.)

(neg.) John DOES NOT spen*d* too much money *every Sunday*.

(int.) DOES John spen*d* too much money *every Sunday?*

Pasado

(af.) John spenT too much money *last Sunday.*
(Juan gastó demasiado dinero el domingo pasado.)

(neg.) John DID NOT spend too much money *last Sunday.*

(int.) DID John spend too much money *last Sunday?*

Antepresente

(af.) They *have* spenT a long time in New York.
(Ellos han pasado mucho tiempo en Nueva York.)

(neg.) They *have* NOT spenT a long time in New York.

(int.) *Have* they spenT a long time in New York?

Ejemplos ilustrativos de cómo emplear el verbo marcado con el número 2 en sus tiempos y formas fundamentales: clasificación *D, T.*

Infinitivo

You have *to send* those orders on time.
(Usted tiene que enviar esos pedidos a tiempo.)

Presente

(af.) We send merchandise to them *every month.*
(Les enviamos mercancía cada mes.)

(neg.) We DO NOT send merchandise to them *every month.*

(int.) DO we send merchandise to them *every month?*

Pasado

(af.) We senT merchandise to them *last month.*
(Les enviamos mercancía el mes pasado.)

(neg.) We DID NOT send merchandise to them *last month.*

(int.) DID we send merchandise to them *last month?*

Antepresente

(af.) He *has* senT them the new catalogue.
(Él les ha enviado el nuevo catálogo.)

(neg.)   He *has* NOT senT them the new catalogue.

(int.)   *Has* he senT them the new catalogue?

Ejemplos ilustrativos de cómo emplear el verbo marcado con el número 3 en sus tiempos y formas fundamentales: clasificación *D, T*.

Infinitivo

He does not like *to* lend his books.
(A él no le gusta prestar sus libros.)

Presente

(af.)   My grandfather lends us money *every month*.
(Mi abuelo nos presta dinero todos los meses.)

(neg.)   My grandfather DOES NOT lend us money *every month*.

(int.)   DOES my grandfather lend us money *every month?*

Pasado

(af.)   My grandfather lenT us money *last month*.
(Mi abuelo nos prestó dinero el mes pasado.)

(neg.)   My grandfather DID NOT lend us money *last month*.

(int.)   DID my grandfather lend us money *last month?*

Antepresente

(af.)   Your parents *have* lenT you their car *lately*.
(Tus padres te han prestado su auto últimamente.)

(neg.)   Your parents *have* NOT lenT you their car *lately*.

(int.)   *Have* your parents lenT you their car *lately?*

Ejemplos ilustrativos de cómo emplear el verbo marcado con el número 4 en sus tiempos y formas fundamentales: clasificación *D, T*.

Infinitivo

He does not want *to* bend his arm.
(Él no quiere doblar el brazo.)

60

Presente

(af.) Mary bends her knee before the altar *every Sunday*.
(María dobla su rodilla ante el altar todos los domingos.)

(neg.) Mary DOES NOT bend her knee before the altar *every Sunday*.

(int.) DOES Mary bend her knee before the altar *every Sunday?*

Pasado

(af.) Mary benT her knee before the altar *last Sunday*.
(María dobló su rodilla ante el altar el domingo pasado.)

(neg.) Mary DID NOT bend her knee before the altar *last Sunday*.

(int.) DID Mary bend her knee before the altar *last Sunday?*

Antepresente

(af.) John *has* benT the branch of that tree.
(Juan ha doblado la rama de ese árbol.)

(neg.) John *has* NOT benT the branch of that tree.

(int.) *Has* John benT the branch of that tree?

Ejemplos ilustrativos de cómo emplear el verbo marcado con el número 5 en sus tiempos y formas fundamentales: clasificación *D, T.*

Infinitivo

That young engineer is going *to* build another bridge.
(Ese joven ingeniero va a construir otro puente.)

Presente

(af.) My father builds many houses *every year*.
(Mi padre construye muchas casas cada año.)

(neg.) My father DOES NOT build many houses *every year*.

(int.) DOES my father build many houses *every year?*

Pasado

(af.)   My father buil*T* many houses *last year.*
(Mi padre construyó muchas casas el año pasado.)

(neg.)   My father DID NOT build many houses *last year.*

(int.)   DID my father build many houses *last year?*

Antepresente

(af.)   They *have* buil*T* a great stadium near the city.
(Ellos han construido un gran estadio cerca de la ciudad.)

(neg.)   They *have* NOT buil*T* a great stadium near the city.

(int.)   *Have* they buil*T* a great stadium near the city?

Clasificación: *I, U*.

Características: Infinitivos cuya vocal única es una *i* (cl*i*ng) que se cambia en *u* (cl*u*ng) para formar su pasado y participio pasado excepto en *to* h*a*ng (colgar). En este grupo la *i* tiene un sonido intermedio entre la *i* y la *e* *(i/e)* y la *u* suena como la *o* castellana. En *to* str*i*ke la *i* se pronuncia *ai*.

Infinitivo	Pasado	Participio Pasado
1. *to* swing (columpiar, me-cer)	sw*U*ng (columpió, meció)	sw*U*ng (columpiado, meci-do)
2. *to* wring (exprimir, torcer)	wr*U*ng (exprimió, torció)	wr*U*ng (exprimido, torcido)
3. *to* cling (pegarse, aferrar-se)	cl*U*ng (se pegó, se aferró)	cl*U*ng (pegado, aferrado)
4. *to* string (enhebrar, ensar-tar)	str*U*ng (enhebró, ensartó)	str*U*ng (enhebrado, ensar-tado)
5. *to* sting (picar, pinchar)	st*U*ng (picó, pinchó)	st*U*ng (picado, pinchado)
6. *to* stick (clavar, pegar)	st*U*ck (clavó, pegó)	st*U*ck (clavado, pegado)
7. *to* strike* (golpear, dar gol-pes)	str*U*ck (golpeó, dio golpes)	str*U*ck (golpeado, dado gol-pes)
8. *to* hang** (colgar)	h*U*ng (colgó)	h*U*ng (colgado)

* El participio pasado también puede ser *stricken* y significa atacado de alguna enfermedad o fuerte emoción negativa: pánico, ira, etc.

** También es verbo regular (hang*ed*) y significa colgar (de ahorcar).

Ejemplos ilustrativos de cómo emplear el verbo marcado con el número 1 en sus tiempos y formas fundamentales: clasificación *I, U*.

Infinitivo

Children like *to* swing in meritots.
(A los niños les gusta mecerse en los columpios.)

Presente

(af.) Mary swings herself on the meritot *every day*.
(María se mece en el columpio todos los días.)

(neg.) Mary DOES NOT swing herself on the meritot *every day*.

(int.) DOES Mary swing herself on the meritot *every day?*

Pasado

(af.) Mary swUng herself on the meritot *yesterday*.
(María se meció en el columpio aver.)

(neg.) Mary DID NOT swing herself on the meritot *yesterday*.

(int.) DID Mary swing herself on the meritot *yesterday?*

Antepresente

(af.) You *have* swUng little John on the meritot *many times*.
(Usted ha mecido al pequeño Juan en el columpio muchas veces.)

(neg.) You *have* NOT swUng little John on the meritot *many times*.

(int.) *Have* you swUng little John on the meritot *many times?*

Ejemplos ilustrativos de cómo emplear el verbo marcado con el número 2 en sus tiempos y formas fundamentales: clasificación *I, U*.

Infinitivo

The maid has *to* wring the clothes.
(La criada tiene que exprimir la ropa.)

Presente

(af.) The woman wrings the clothes *every day*.
(La mujer exprime la ropa todos los días.)

(neg.) The woman DOES NOT wring the clothes *every day*.

(int.) DOES the woman wring the clothes *every day?*

Pasado

(af.) The woman wr*U*ng the clothes *yesterday*.
(La mujer exprimió la ropa ayer.)

(neg.) The woman DID NOT wring the clothes *yesterday*.

(int.) DID the woman wring the clothes *yesterday?*

Antepresente

(af.) This washing-machine *has* wr*U*ng the clothes automatically.
(Esta lavadora ha exprimido la ropa automáticamente.)

(neg.) This washing-machine *has* NOT wr*U*ng the clothes automatically.

(int.) *Has* this washing-machine wr*U*ng the clothes automatically?

Ejemplos ilustrativos de cómo emplear el verbo marcado con el número 3 en sus tiempos y formas fundamentales: clasificación *I, U*.

Infinitivo

He likes *to* cling to the idea that he is self-sufficient.
(Le gusta aferrarse a la idea de que es auto-suficiente.)

Presente

(af.) These little puppies cling to their mother at feeding time.
(Estos perritos se pegan a su madre a la hora del alimento.)

(neg.) These little puppies DO NOT cling to their mother at feeding time.

(int.)   DO these little puppies cling to their mother at feeding time?

Pasado

(af.)   These little puppies clUng to their mother at feeding time.
(Estos perritos se pegaron a su madre a la hora del alimento.)

(neg.)   These little puppies DID NOT cling to their mother at feeding time.

(int.)   DID these little puppies cling to their mother at feeding time?

Antepresente

(af.)   Little Mary *has* clUng to her mother's lap during storms.
(La pequeña María se ha pegado al regazo de su madre durante la tormenta.)

(neg.)   Little Mary *has* NOT clUng to her mother's lap during storms.

(int.)   *Has* little Mary clUng to her mother's lap during storms?

Ejemplos ilustrativos de cómo emplear el verbo marcado con el número 4 en sus tiempos y formas fundamentales: clasificación *I, U*.

Infinitivo

You have *to* string the thread carefully.
(Usted tiene que enhebrar el hilo con cuidado.)

Presente

(af.)   The women string the thread in the factory *every day*.
(Las mujeres enhebran el hilo en la fábrica todos los días.)

(neg.)   The woman DO NOT string the thread in the factory *every day*.

(int.)   DO the woman string the thread in the factory *every day*?

Pasado

(af.)   The women strUng the thread in the factory *yesterday*.
(Las mujeres enhebraron el hilo en la fábrica ayer.)

(neg.) The women DID NOT string the thread in the factory *yesterday*.

(int.) DID the women string the thread in the factory *yesterday?*

Antepresente

(af.)   She *has* strUng many beads *lately*.
(Ella ha ensartado muchas cuentas últimamente.)

(neg.) She *has* NOT strUng many beads *lately*.

(int.) *Has* she strUng many beads *lately?*

Ejemplos ilustrativos de cómo emplear el verbo marcado con el número 5 en sus tiempos y formas fundamentales: clasificación *I, U*.

Infinitivo

Those bees are going *to* sting you, if you keep on bothering them.
(Esas abejas van a picarte, si sigues molestándolas.)

Presente

(af.)   These mosquitoes sting me *every night*.
(Estos mosquitos me pican todas las noches.)

(neg.) These mosquitoes DO NOT sting me *every night*.

(int.) DO these mosquitoes sting me *every night?*

Pasado

(af.)   These mosquitoes stUng me *last night*.
(Estos mosquitos me picaron anoche.)

(neg.) These mosquitoes DID NOT sting me *last night*.

(int.) DID these mosquitoes sting me *last night?*

Antepresente

(af.)   Those poisonous snakes *have* st*U*ng many people *lately*.
(Esas serpientes venenosas han picado a mucha gente
últimamente.)

(neg.) Those poisonous snakes *have* NOT st*U*ng many people
lately.

(int.) *Have* those poisonous snakes st*U*ng many people *lately?*

Ejemplos ilustrativos de cómo emplear el verbo marcado con
el número 6 en sus tiempos y formas fundamentales: clasificación *I*, *U*.

Infinitivo

John does not have *to* stick chewing-gum on his desk.
(Juan no tiene que pegar chicle en su pupitre.)

Presente

(af.)   He sticks nails on boards *every day*.
(Él clava clavos en tablas todos los días.)

(neg.) He DOES NOT stick nails on boards *every day*.

(int.) DOES he stick nails on boards *every day?*

Pasado

(af.)   He st*U*ck nails on boards *yesterday*.
(Él clavó clavos en tablas ayer.)

(neg.) He DID NOT stick nails on boards *yesterday*.

(int.) DID he stick nails on boards *yesterday?*

Antepresente

(af.)   They *have* st*U*ck many labels on beer-bottles.
(Ellos han pegado muchas etiquetas en botellas de cer-
veza.)

(neg.) They *have* NOT st*U*ck many labels on beer-bottles.

(int.) *Have* they' st*U*ck many labels on beer-bottles?

Ejemplos ilustrativos de cómo emplear el verbo marcado con el número 7 en sus tiempos y formas fundamentales: clasificación *I, U*.

Infinitivo

Charles like *to* strike with a stick at his classmates in school.
(A Carlos le gusta dar golpes con un palo a sus compañeros de clases en la escuela.)

Presente

(af.)   These boys strike at the orange-tree *every year*.
(Estos muchachos golpean al naranjo cada año.)

(neg.)   These boys DO NOT strike at the orange-tree *every year*.

(int.)   DO these boys strike at the orange-tree *every year?*

Pasado

(af.)   These boys str*U*ck at the orange-tree *last year*.
(Estos muchachos golpearon al naranjo el año pasado.)

(neg.)   These boys DID NOT stri*ck* at the orange-tree *last year*.

(int.)   DID these boys strick at the orange-tree *last year?*

Antepresente

(af.)   He *has* str*U*ck at the donkeys *many times*.
Él ha golpeado a los burros muchas veces.

(neg.)   He *has* NOT str*U*ck at the donkeys *many times*.

(int.)   *Has* he str*U*ck at the donkeys *many times?*

Ejemplos ilustrativos de cómo emplear el verbo marcado con el número 8 en sus tiempos y formas fundamentales: clasificación *I, U*.

Infinitivo

She has *to* hang her clothes *every day*.
(Ella tiene que colgar su ropa todos los días.)

Presente

(af.)   The woman hangs the clothes after the washing.
(La mujer cuelga la ropa después del lavado.)

(neg.)   The woman DOES NOT hang the clothes after the washing.

(int.)   DOES the woman hang the clothes after the washing?

Pasado

(af.)   The woman hUng the clothes after the washing.
(La mujer colgó la ropa después del lavado.)

(neg.)   The woman DID NOT hang the clothes after the washing.

(int.)   DID the woman hang the clothes after the washing?

Antepresente

(af.)   She *has* hUng the picture *upon* a nail.
(Ella ha colgado el cuadro de un clavo.)

(neg.)   She *has* NOT hUng the picture *upon* a nail.

(int.)   *Has* she hUng the picture *upon* a nail?

Clasificación: *AY, AID*

Características: La terminación *ay* es la característica de todos los infinitivos pertenecientes a este grupo (to p*ay*). En el pasado y participio pasado dicha terminación *ay* se cambia por *aid* (p*aid*). La fonética de *ay* es *ei* y *aid* se pronuncia *eid*, excepto en *said* (pronúnciese *sed*).

	Infinitivo	Pasado	Participio Pasado
1.	to s*ay* (decir)	s*AID* (dijo)	s*AID* (dicho)
2.	to p*ay* (pagar)	p*AID* (pagó)	p*AID* (pagado)
3.	to l*ay* (colocar, poner huevos)	l*AID* (colocó, puso huevos)	l*AID* (colocado, puesto huevos)

Ejemplos ilustrativos de cómo emplear el verbo marcado con el número 1 en sus tiempos y formas fundamentales: clasificación *AY, AID*.

Infinitivo

What are you trying *to say?*
(¿Qué está usted tratando de decir?)

Presente

(af.) Peter s*ay*s good night before going to bed.
(Pedro dice buenas noches antes de acostarse.)

(neg.) Peter DOES NOT say good night before going to bed.

(int.) DOES Peter s*ay* good night before going to bed?

Pasado

(af.) Peter s*AID* good night to us *last night*.
(Pedro nos dijo buenas noches anoche.)

71

(neg.) Peter DID NOT say good night to us *last night.*

(int.) DID Peter say good night to us *last night?*

Antepresente

(af.) The newspapers *have* s*AID* many things about him.
(Los periódicos han dicho muchas cosas de él.)

(neg.) The newspapers *have* NOT s*AID* many things about him.

(int.) *Have* the newspapers s*AID* many things about him?

Ejemplos ilustrativos de cómo emplear el verbo marcado con el número 2 en sus tiempos y formas fundamentales: clasificación *AY, AID.*

Infinitivo

We have *to pay* this bill immediately.
(Tenemos que pagar esta cuenta inmediatamente.)

Presente

(af.) They *pay* their bills *every month.*
(Ellos pagan sus cuentas todos los meses.)

(neg.) They DO NOT *pay* their bills *every month.*

(int.) DO they *pay* their bills *every month?*

Pasado

(af.) They p*AID* their bills *last month.*
(Ellos pagaron sus cuentas el mes pasado.)

(neg.) They DID NOT *pay* their bills *last month.*

(int.) DID they *pay* their bills *last month?*

Antepresente

(af.) My uncle *has* p*AID* too much for that house.
(Mi tío ha pagado demasiado por esa casa.)

(neg.) My uncle *has* NOT p*AID* too much for that house.

(int.) *Has* my uncle p*AID* too much for that house?

Ejemplos ilustrativos de cómo emplear el verbo marcado con el número 3 en sus tiempos y formas fundamentales: clasificación *AY, AID*.

Infinitivo

That brown hen is going *to* lay an egg soon.
(Esa gallina parda va a poner un huevo pronto.)

Presente

(af.)   My hens l*ay* eggs *every day*.
(Mis gallinas ponen huevos todos los días.)

(neg.)   My hens DO NOT l*ay* eggs *every day*.

(int.)   DO my hens l*ay* eggs *every day?*

Pasado

(af.)   That white hen l*AID* many eggs *last month*.
(Esa gallina blanca puso muchos huevos el mes pasado.)

(neg.)   That white hen DID NOT l*ay* many eggs *last month*.

(int.)   DID that white hen l*ay* many eggs *last month?*

Antepresente

(af.)   The president *has* l*AID* the first stone of that hospital.
(El presidente ha colocado la primera piedra de ese hospital).

(neg.)   The president *has* NOT l*AID* the first stone of that hospital.

(int.)   *Has* the presidente l*AID* the first stone of that hospital?

Clasificación: *IND, OUND.*

Características: Obsérvese que la combinación *ind,* que es rasgo común en los infinitivos, se transforma en *ound* para formar el pasado y participio pasado de esta clasificación. La fonética de *ind* es *áind* y la de *ound* es *áund.*

Infinitivo	Pasado	Participio Pasado
1. *to* f*ind* (encontrar)	f*OUND* (encontró)	f*OUND* (encontrado)
2. *to* b*ind* (unir, atar)	b*OUND* (unió, ató)	b*OUND* (unido, atado)
3. *to* g*rind* (triturar, moler)	gr*OUND* (trituró, molió).	gr*OUND* (triturado, molido)
4. *to* w*ind* (dar cuerda, enrollar)	w*OUND* (dio cuerda, enrolló)	w*OUND* (dado cuerda, enrollado)

Ejemplos ilustrativos de cómo emplear el verbo marcado con el número 1 en sus tiempos y formas fundamentales: clasificación *IND, OUND.*

Infinitivo

I am trying *to* f*ind* a bigger apartment.
(Estoy tratando de encontrar un departamento más grande.)

Presente

(af.) Archeologists f*ind* interesting things in those ruins.
(Los arqueólogos encuentran cosas interesantes en esas ruinas.)

(neg.) Archeologists DO NOT f*ind* interesting things in those ruins.

(int.) DO archeologists f*ind* interesting things in those ruins?

74

Pasado

(af.) My brother f*OUND* fifty dollars on the street.
(Mi hermano encontró cincuenta dólares en la calle.)

(neg.) My brother DID NOT find fifty dollars on the street.

(int.) DID my brother find fifty dollars on the street?

Antepresente

(af.) She *has* f*OUND* many mistakes in that writing.
(Ella ha encontrado muchos errores en ese escrito.)

(neg.) She *has* NOT f*OUND* many mistakes in that writing.

(int.) *Has* she f*OUND* many mistakes in that writing?

Ejemplos ilustrativos de cómo emplear el verbo marcado con el número 2 en sus tiempos y formas fundamentales: clasificación *IND, OUND*.

Infinitivo

You have *to* b*ind* everything very tightly.
(Usted tiene que unir todo muy fuertemente.)

Presente

(af.) He b*ind*s all the bundles together *every day*.
(Él ata todos los bultos juntos todos los días.)

(neg.) He DOES NOT b*ind* all the bundles together *every day*.

(int.) DOES he b*ind* all the bundles together *every day?*

Pasado

(af.) He b*OUND* all the bundles together *yesterday*.
(Él ató todos los bultos juntos ayer.)

(neg.) He DID NOT b*ind* all the bundles together *yesterday*.

(int.) DID he b*ind* all the bundles together *yesterday?*

Antepresente

(af.) They *have* b*OUND* all those sticks in one bundle.
(Ellos han atado todas esas varas en un montón.)

(neg.)   They *have* NOT b*OUND* all those sticks in one bundle.
(int.)   *Have* they b*OUND* all those sticks in one bundle?

Ejemplos ilustrativos de cómo emplear el verbo marcado con el número 3 en sus tiempos y formas fundamentales: clasificación *IND, OUND.*

Infinitivo

She will have *to* gr*ind* that corn very well.
(Ella tendrá que moler ese maíz muy bien.)

Presente

(af.)   That woman gr*ind*s corn *every day.*
        (Esa mujer muele maíz todos los días.)
(neg.)   That woman DOES NOT gr*ind* corn *every day.*
(int.)   DOES that woman gr*ind* corn *every day?*

Pasado

(af.)   That woman gr*OUND* all the corn *yesterday.*
        (Esa mujer molió todo el maíz ayer.)
(neg.)   That woman DID NOT gr*ind* all the corn *yesterday.*
(int.)   DID that woman gr*ind* all the corn *yesterday?*

Antepresente

(af.)   He *has* gr*OUND* many things with that machine.
        (Él ha triturado muchas cosas con esa máquina.)
(neg.)   He *has* NOT gr*OUND* many things with that machine.
(int.)   *Has* he gr*OUND* many things with that machine?

Ejemplos ilustrativos de cómo emplear el verbo marcado con el número 4 en sus tiempos y formas fundamentales: clasificación *IND, OUND.*

Infinitivo

Do not forget *to* w*ind* the clock *every night.*
(No olvides dar cuerda al reloj de pared todas las noches.)

Presente

(af.)   Peter winds his watch before going to bed.
        (Pedro da cuerda a su reloj antes de acostarse.)

(neg.) Peter DOES NOT wind his watch before going to bed.

(int.) DOES Peter wind his watch before going to bed?

Pasado

(af.)   Peter wOUND his watch before going to bed.
        (Pedro dio cuerda a su reloj antes de acostarse.)

(neg.) Peter DID NOT wind his watch before going to bed.

(int.) DID Peter wind his watch before going to bed?

Antepresente

(af.)   Frank has wOUND the big clock many times.
        (Paco le ha dado cuerda al reloj grande muchas veces.)

(neg.) Frank has NOT wOUND the big clock many times.

(int.) Has Frank wOUND the big clock many times?

Clasificación: *ELL, OLD.*

Características: La terminación del infinitivo *ell* (to *tell*) se cambia por *old* (t*old*) en el pasado y participio pasado. Fonética: *ell* se pronuncia *el* y *old* suena *ould*.

	Infinitivo	Pasado	Participio Pasado
1.	to t*ell* (decir, contar)	t*OLD* (dijo, contó)	t*OLD* (dicho, contado)
2.	to foret*ell* (predecir)	foret*OLD* (predijo)	foret*OLD* (predicho)
3.	to s*ell* (vender)	s*OLD* (vendió)	s*OLD* (vendido)

Ejemplos ilustrativos de cómo emplear el verbo marcado con el número 1 en sus tiempos y formas fundamentales: clasificación *ELL, OLD.*

Infinitivo

What do you intend *to tell* your parents?
(¿Qué tienes pensado decir a tus padres?)

Presente

(af.)   My father t*ell*s us to study.
(Mi padre nos dice que estudiemos.)

(neg.)   My father DOES NOT t*ell* us to study.

(int.)   DOES my father t*ell* us to study?

Pasado

(af.)   My father t*OLD* us to study.
(Mi padre nos dijo que estudiáramos.)

(neg.)   My father DID NOT t*ell* us to study.

(int.)   DID my father t*ell* us to study?

Antepresente

(af.) She *has* t*OLD* him many things about her trip.
(Ella le ha contado a él muchas cosas acerca de su viaje.)

(neg.) She *has* NOT t*OLD* him many things about her trip.

(int.) *Has* she t*OLD* him many things about her trip?

Ejemplos ilustrativos de cómo emplear el verbo marcado con el número 2 en sus tiempos y formas fundamentales: clasificación *ELL, OLD.*

Infinitivo

Fortune-tellers pretend *to* foret*ell* future events.
(Los adivinadores pretenden predecir acontecimientos futuros.)

Presente

(af.) That gipsy foret*ell*s the fortune.
(Esa gitana predice la suerte.)

(neg.) That gipsy DOES NOT foret*ell* the fortune.

(int.) DOES that gipsy foret*ell* the fortune?

Pasado

(af.) That famous astrologist foret*OLD* that disaster *last year*.
(Ese astrólogo famoso predijo ese desastre el año pasado.)

(neg.) That famous astrologist DID NOT foret*ell* that disaster *last year*.

(int.) DID that famous astrologist foret*ell* that disaster *last year?*

Antepresente

(af.) Prophets *have* foret*OLD* the end of the world.
(Los profetas han predicho el fin del mundo.)

(neg.) Prophets *have* NOT foret*OLD* the end of the world.

(int.) *Have* prophets foret*OLD* the end of the world?

Ejemplos ilustrativos de cómo emplear el verbo marcado con el número 3 en sus tiempos y formas fundamentales: clasificación *ELL, OLD*.

Infinitivo

They have *to sell* that merchandise as soon as possible. (Ellos tienen que vender esa mercancía tan pronto como sea posible.)

Presente

(af.) They *sell* their products in Latin America.
(Ellos venden sus productos en América Latina.)

(neg.) They DO NOT *sell* their products in Latin America.

(int.) DO they *sell* their products in Latin America?

Pasado

(af.) They s*OLD* their products in Latin America.
(Ellos vendieron sus productos en América Latina.)

(neg.) They DID NOT *sell* their products in Latin America.

(int.) DID they *sell* their products in Latin America?

Antepresente

(af.) France *has* s*OLD* machinery to Mexico *lately*.
(Francia ha vendido maquinaria a México últimamente.)

(neg.) France *has* NOT s*OLD* machinery to Mexico *lately*.

(int.) *Has* France s*OLD* machinery to Mexico *lately?*

Clasificación: *STAND, STOOD.*

Características: La terminación *stand* del infinitivo se cambia por *stood* en el pasado y participio pasado. *Stood* se pronuncia *stud.*

Infinitivo	Pasado	Participio pasado
1. to stand (quedarse, estar de pie)	STOOD (se quedó, estuvo de pie)	STOOD (quedado, estado de pie)
2. to understand (entender)	underSTOOD (entendió)	underSTOOD (entendido)
3. to withstand (resistir, oponer)	withSTOOD (resistió, opuso)	withSTOOD (resistido, opuesto)

Ejemplos ilustrativos de cómo emplear el verbo marcado con el número 1 en sus tiempos y formas fundamentales: clasificación *STAND, STOOD.*

Infinitivo

John likes *to stand* near the entrance.
(A Juan le gusta quedarse cerca de la entrada.)

Presente

(af.) John *stand*s on his feet in a crowded bus.
(Juan se queda de pie en un autobús atestado.)

(neg.) John DOES NOT *stand* on his feet in a crowded bus.

(int.) DOES John *stand* on his feet in a crowded bus?

Pasado

(af.) The pupils *STOOD* up when the teacher entered the clasroom.
(Los alumnos se pusieron de pie cuando el maestro entró al aula.)

81

(neg.)   The pupils DID NOT *stand* up when the teacher entered the classroom.

(int.)   DID the pupils *stand* up when the teacher entered the classroom?

Antepresente

(af.)   Those students *have STOOD* up before the Mexican flag.
(Esos estudiantes se han puesto de pie ante la bandera mexicana.)

(neg.)   Those students *have* NOT *STOOD* up before the Mexican flag.

(int.)   *Have* those students *STOOD* up before the Mexican flag?

Ejemplos ilustrativos de cómo emplear el verbo marcado con el número 2 en sus tiempos y formas fundamentales clasificación *STAND, STOOD.*

Infinitivo

He has *to* under*stand* certain things.
(Él tiene que entender ciertas cosas.)

Presente

(af.)   He under*stands* English well.
(Él entiende inglés bien.)

(neg.)   He DOES NOT under*stand* English well.

(int.)   DOES he under*stand* English well?

Pasado

(af.)   They under*STOOD* the explanation *yesterday.*
(Ellos comprendieron la explicación ayer.)

(neg.)   They DID NOT under*stand* the explanation *yesterday.*

(int.)   DID they under*stand* the explanation *yesterday?*

Antepresente

(af.)   You *have* unders*STOOD* me.
(Usted me ha comprendido.)

(neg.) You *have* NOT under*STOOD* me.

(int.) *Have* you under*STOOD* me?

Ejemplos ilustrativos de cómo emplear el verbo marcado con
el número 3 en sus tiempos y formas fundamentales: clasificación *STAND, STOOD.*

Infinitivo

This ship has *to* with*stand* the storm.
(Este barco tiene que resistir la tormenta.)

Presente

(af.) That man with*stands* to every kind of violence.
(Ese hombre se opone a toda clase de violencia.)

(neg.) That man DOES NOT with*stand* to every kind of
violence.

(int.) DOES that man with*stand* to every kind of violence?

Pasado

(af.) That people with*STOOD* the foreign aggression.
(Ese pueblo resistió la agresión extranjera.)

(neg.) That people DID NOT with*stand* the foreign aggression.

(int.) DID that people with*stand* the foreign aggression?

Antepresente

(af.) That small nation *has* with*STOOD* the economic aggression.
(Esa pequeña nación ha resistido la agresión económica.)

(neg.) That small nation *has* NOT with*STOOD* the economic
aggression.

(int.) *Has* that small nation withSTOOD the economic aggression?

Clasificación: *OLD, ELD.*

Características: La combinación *old* del infinitivo se cambia en *eld* para formar el pasado y participio pasado. La fonética de *old* es *óuld* y la de *eld* igual como se escribe

Infinitivo	Pasado	Participio Pasado
1. *to* ho*ld* (sostener, sujetar)	hELD (sostuvo, sujetó)	hELD (sostenido, sujetado)
2. *to* beho*ld* (contemplar)	behELD (contempló)	behELD (contemplado)
3. *to* withho*ld* (retener).	withhELD (retuvo)	withhELD (retenido)

Ejemplos ilustrativos de cómo emplear el verbo marcado con el número 1 en sus tiempos y formas fundamentales: clasificación *OLD, ELD.*

Infinitivo

Mary likes *to* ho*ld* long conversations over the telephone. (A María le gusta sostener largas conversaciones por teléfono.)

Presente

(af.) John ho*ld*s Mary's books on their way to school. (Juan sostiene los libros de María camino de la escuela.)

(neg.) John DOES NOT ho*ld* Mary's books on their way to school.

(int.) DOES John ho*ld* Mary's books on their way to school?

Pasado

(af.) She hELD the baby in her arms *yesterday.* (Ella sostuvo al bebé en sus brazos ayer.

(neg.) She DID NOT ho*ld* the baby in her arms *yesterday.*

(int.) DID she ho*ld* the baby in her arms *yesterday?*

84

Antepresente

(af.)   They *have* h*ELD* different theories on Mars.
(Ellos han sostenido diferentes teorías sobre Marte.)

(neg.) They *have* NOT h*ELD* different theories on Mars.

(int.) *Have* they h*ELD* different theories on Mars?

Ejemplos ilustrativos de cómo emplear el verbo marcado con el número 2 en sus tiempos y formas fundamentales: clasificación *OLD, ELD.*

Infinitivo

She likes *to* beh*old* that beautiful scenery.
(A ella le gusta contemplar ese bello paisaje.)

Presente

(af.)   She beh*old*s the sunset *every afternoon.*
(Ella contempla la puesta del sol todas las tardes.)

(neg.) She DOES NOT beh*old* the sunset *every afternoon.*

(int.) DOES she beh*old* the sunset *every afternoon?*

Pasado

(af.)   My parents beh*ELD* the view of Paris from the Eiffel Tower.
(Mis padres contemplaron la vista de París desde la Torre Eiffel.)

(neg.) My parents DID NOT beh*old* the view of Paris from the Eiffel Tower.

(int.) DID my parents beh*old* the view of Paris from the Eiffel Tower?

Antepresente

(af.)   He *has* beh*ELD* that picture *many times.*
(Él ha contemplado ese cuadro muchas veces.)

(neg.) He *has* NOT beh*ELD* that picture *many times.*

(int.) *Has* he beh*ELD* that picture *many times?*

Ejemplos ilustrativos de cómo emplear el verbo marcado con el número 3 en sus tiempos y formas fundamentales: clasificación *OLD, ELD.*

Infinitivo

He does not have *to* withh*old* my salary.
(Él no tiene por qué retener mi sueldo.)

Presente

(af.)   My employer withh*olds* my income-tax *every month.*
(Mi patrón retiene mis impuestos sobre la renta todos los meses.)

(neg.)   My employer DOES NOT withh*old* my income-tax *every month*

(int.)   DOES my employer withh*old* my income-tax *every month?*

Pasado

(af.)   The immigration service withh*ELD* our passports.
(El servicio de inmigración retuvo nuestros pasaportes.)

(neg.)   The immigration service DID NOT withh*eld* our passports.

(int.)   DID the immigration service withh*eld our passports?*

Antepresente

(af.)   The inspector *has* withh*ELD* those documents.
(El inspector ha retenido esos documentos.)

(neg.)   The inspector *has* NOT withh*ELD* those documents.

(int.)   *Has* the inspector withh*ELD* those documents?

Clasificación: *I-E, ID* o *IT*.

Características: Obsérvese que entre las vocales *i-e* se interpone la consonante *t* o *d (to bite, to hide)* en todos los infinitivos excepto en *to light*. En el pasado y participio pasado, la vocal *e* se elimina *(bit, hid)*.

La *i* del infinitivo tiene sonido de *ai* y la *e* es muda. En el pasado y participio pasado la *i* suena como en español.

Infinitivo	*Pasado*	*Participio Pasado*
1. *to* hid*e* (esconder)	h*I*D (escondió)	h*I*D* (escondido)
2. *to* sl*i*d*e* (deslizar, resba- lar)	sl*I*D (deslizó, resbaló)	sl*I*D* (deslizado, resbalado)
3. *to* chid*e* (reprender)	ch*I*D (reprendió)	ch*I*D* (reprendido)
4. *to* bite (morder, picar)	b*I*T (mordió, picó)	b*I*T* (mordido, picado)
5. *to* light (encender)	l*I*T (encendió)	l*I*T (encendido)

* Sus participios pasados también pueden ser: hi*dden*, sli*dden*, chi*dden* y bi*tten* respectivamente, y cuya *i* tiene el mismo sonido que en castellano.

Ejemplos ilustrativos de cómo emplear el verbo marcado con el número 1 en sus tiempos y formas fundamentales: clasificación *I-E, ID* o *IT*.

Infinitivo

What are you trying *to* hid*e*?
(¿Qué estás tratando de esconder?)

Presente

(af.)   Charles hid*es* from his friends *every day*.
(Carlos se esconde de sus amigos todos los días.)

(neg.) Charles DOES NOT h*ide* from his friends *every day*.

(int.) DOES Charles h*ide* from his friends *every day?*

Pasado

(af.) The thief h*ID* from the police.
(El ladrón se escondió de la policía.)

(neg.) The thief DID NOT h*ide* from the police.

(int.) DID the thief h*ide* from the police?

Antepresente

(af.) He *has* h*ID* (h*idden*) his money under the mattress.
(Él ha escondido su dinero debajo del colchón.)

(neg.) He *has* NOT h*ID* (h*idden*) his money under mattress.

(int.) *Has* he h*ID* (h*idden*) his money under the mattress?

Ejemplos ilustrativos de cómo emplear el verbo marcado con el número 2 en sus tiempos y formas fundamentales: clasificación *I-E, ID* o *IT*.

Infinitivo

Eskimos like *to* sl*ide* on their sleighs.
(A los esquimales les gusta deslizarse en sus trineos.)

Presente

(af.) That sleigh sl*ides* swiftly on the snow.
(Ese trineo se desliza rápidamente en la nieve.)

(neg.) That sleigh DOES NOT sl*ide* swiftly on the snow.

int.) DOES that sleigh sl*ide* swiftly on the snow?

Pasado

(af.) That sleigh sl*ID* swiftly on the snow *yesterday*.
(Ese trineo se deslizó rápidamente en la nieve ayer.)

(neg.) That sleigh DID NOT sl*ide* swiftly on the snow.

(int.) DID that sleigh sl*ide* swiftly on the snow *yesterday?*

(af.)   You *have* slID (sl*idden*) because of this slippery floor.
(Usted ha resbalado debido a este piso resbaloso.)

(neg.) You *have* NOT slID (sl*idden*) because of this slippery
floor.

(int.) *Have* you slID (sl*idden*) because of this slippery floor?

Ejemplos ilustrativos de cómo emplear el verbo marcado con
el número 3 en sus tiempos y formas fundamentales: clasificación *I-E, ID* o *IT.*

Infinitivo

The teacher does not like *to* ch*ide* his pupils.
(Al maestro no le gusta reprender a sus alumnos.)

Presente

(af.)   The teacher ch*ides* the mischievous pupils *every day.*
(El maestro reprende a los alumnos traviesos todos
los días.)

(neg.) The teacher DOES NOT ch*ide* the mischievous pupils
every day.

(int.) DOES the teacher ch*ide* the mischievous pupils *every
day?*

Pasado

(af.)   The teacher ch*ID* a mischievous pupil *yesterday.*
(El maestro regañó a un alumno travieso ayer.)

(neg.) The teacher DID NOT ch*ide* a mischievous pupil
yesterday.

(int.) DID the teacher ch*ide* a mischievous pupil *yesterday?*

Antepresente

(af.)   The teacher *has* ch*ID* (ch*idden*) them many times.
(El maestro los ha reprendido muchas veces.)

(neg.) The teacher *has* NOT ch*ID* (ch*idden*) them many times.

(int.) *Has* the teacher ch*ID* (ch*idden*) them many times?

Ejemplos ilustrativos de cómo emplear el verbo marcado con el número 4 en sus tiempos y formas fundamentales: clasificación *I-E, ID* o *IT*.

Infinitivo

That dog is going *to* bi*te* you, if you keep on bothering him.
(Ese perro va a morderte si sigues molestándolo.)

Presente

(af.) The mosquitoes bi*te* him *every night.*
(Los mosquitos lo pican todas las noches.)

(neg.) The mosquitoes DO NOT bi*te* him *every night.*

(int.) DO the mosquitoes bi*te* him *every night?*

Pasado

(af.) A mad dog b*IT* Charles *last year.*
(Un perro rabioso mordió a Carlos el año pasado.)

(neg.) A mad dog DID NOT bi*te* Charles *last year.*

(int.) DID a mad dog bi*te* Charles *last year?*

Antepresente

(af.) Mosquitoes *have* b*IT* (bi*tt*en) them *many times.*
(Los mosquitos los han picado muchas veces.)

(neg.) Mosquitoes *have* NOT b*IT* (bi*tt*en) them *many times.*

(int.) *Have* mosquitoes b*IT* (bi*tt*en) them *many times?*

Ejemplos ilustrativos de cómo emplear el verbo marcado con el número 5 en sus tiempos y formas fundamentales: clasificación *I-E, ID* o *IT*.

Infinitivo

He does not have *to* light his cigarette near the gasoline can.
(Él no tiene que encender su cigarrillo cerca de la lata de gasolina.)

Presente

(af.) My father lights his cigarettes with a new lighter.
(Mi padre enciende sus cigarrillos con un encendedor nuevo.)

(neg.) My father DOES NOT light his cigarettes with a new lighter.

(int.) DOES my father light his cigarettes with a new lighter?

Pasado

(af.) Mr. Brown *lIT* his pipe with a match *yesterday.*
(El señor Brown encendió su pipa con un cerillo ayer.)

(neg.) Mr. Brown DID NOT light his pipe with a match *yesterday.*

(int.) DID Mr. Brown light his pipe with a match *yesterday?*

Antepresente

(af.) They *have lIT* their cigars with wooden matches.
(Ellos han encendido sus puros con cerillos de madera.)

(neg.) They *have* NOT *lIT* their cigars with wooden matches.

(int.) *Have* they *lIT* thier cigars with wooden matches?

Clasificación: *O,O.*

Características: Observe que el único rasgo que caracteriza a esta agrupación verbal es la vocal *o*, la cual es común en todos ellos tanto en el pasado como en el participio pasado. Por otra parte, también se advertirá que su infinitivo es distinto.

En cuanto a la fonética de los infinitivos, la *o* de *lose* tiene sonido de *u* y la *e* final es muda. En *shoot* la doble *o* suena como *u*. En *shine*, la *i* se pronuncia *ai* y la vocal *a* de *wake* suena *ei*, siendo muda su *e* final.

Tanto los pasados y participios pasados se pronuncian como se escriben, salvo los que constan de *e* finales que son mudas.

	Infinitivo	Pasado	Participio Pasado
1.	*to* win (ganar)	wOn (ganó)	wOn (ganado)
2.	*to* lose (perder)	lOst (perdió)	lOst (perdido)
3.	*to* shoot (disparar)	shOt (disparó)	shOt (disparado)
4.	*to* shine (brillar)	shOne* (brilló)	shOne* (brillado)
5.	*to* wake (despertar)	wOke (despertó)	wOke (despertado)

* Empléase la forma regular shin*ed* en el pasado y participio pasado de *shine*, cuando éste implica *lustrar zapatos*.

Ejemplos ilustrativos de cómo emplear el verbo marcado con el número 1 en sus tiempos y formas fundamentales: clasificación *O, O*.

Infinitivo

They will try *to* win the next foot-ball game.
(Ellos tratarán de ganar el próximo juego de foot-ball.)

Presente

(af.)   Those players win all the games *every year*.
(Esos jugadores ganan todos los juegos todos los años.)

(neg.) Those players DO NOT win all the games *every year*.

(int.) DO those players win all the games *every year?*

Pasado

(af.)   He wOn the world's championship *last year*.
(Él ganó el campeonato mundial el año pasado.)

(neg.) He DID NOT *win* the world's championship *last year*.

(int.) DID he *win* the world's championship *last year?*

Antepresente

(af.)   Mary *has* wOn many beauty contests.
(María ha ganado muchos concursos de belleza.)

(neg.) Mary *has* NOT wOn many beauty contests.

(int.) *Has* Mary wOn many beauty contests?

Ejemplos ilustrativos de cómo emplear el verbo marcado con el número 2 en sus tiempos y formas fundamentales: clasificación O, O.

Infinitivo

You are not going *to* lose money in that investment.
(Usted no va a perder dinero en esa inversión.)

Presente

(af.)   They lose money in those business *every year*.
(Ellos pierden dinero en esos negocios todos los años.)

(neg.) They DO NOT lose money in those business *every year*.

(int.) DO they lose money in those business *every year?*

Pasado

(af.)   Charles lOst his English book *last week*.
(Carlos perdió su libro de inglés la semana pasada.)

93

(neg.) Charles DID NOT *lose* his English book *last week.*

(int.) DID Charles *lose* his English book *last week?*

Antepresente

(af.) They *have* lOst many games *during this season.*
(Ellos han perdido muchos partidos durante esta temporada.)

(neg.) They *have* NOT lOst many games *during this season.*

(int.) *Have* they lOst many games *during this season?*

Ejemplos ilustrativos de cómo emplear el verbo marcado con el número 3 en sus tiempos y formas fundamentales. Clasificación: *O, O*

Infinitivo

They like *to* shoot at the birds in the country.
(A ellos les gusta disparar a las aves en el campo.)

Presente

(af.) Robert shoots at pigeons *every week.*
(Roberto le dispara a las palomas cada semana.)

(neg.) Robert DOES NOT shoot at pigeons *every week.*

(int.) DOES Robert shoot at pigeons *every week?*

Pasado

(af.) They shOt at a tiger in the jungle.
(Ellos le dispararon a un tigre en la selva.)

(neg.) They DID NOT *shoot* at a tiger in the jungle.

(int.) DID they *shoot* at a tiger in the jungle?

Antepresente

(af.) Those hunters *have* shOt at many animals.
(Esos cazadores le han disparado a muchos animales.)

(neg.)   Those hunters *have* NOT sh*O*t at many animales.

(int.)   *Have* those hunters sh*O*t at many animals?

Ejemplos ilustrativos de cómo emplear el verbo marcado con el número 4 en sus tiempos y formas fundamentales: clasificación *O, O*.

Infinitivo

The sun is going *to* shine soon.
(El sol va a brillar pronto.)

Presente

(af.)   The sun shines *every day*.
(El sol brilla todos los días.)

(neg.)   The sun DOES NOT shine *every day*.

(int.)   DOES the sun shine *every day?*

Pasado

(af.)   The sun sh*O*ne very brightly *yesterday*.
(El sol brilló muy refulgentemente ayer.)

(neg.)   The sun DID NOT *shine* very brightly *yesterday*.

(int.)   DID the sun *shine* very brightly *yesterday?*

Antepresente

(af.)   The sun *has* sh*O*ne every day *this Summer*.
(El sol ha brillado todos los días este verano.)

(neg.)   The sun *has* NOT sh*O*ne every day *this Summer*.

(int.)   *Has* the sun sh*O*ne every day *this Summer?*

Ejemplos ilustrativos de cómo emplear el verbo marcado con el número 5 en sus tiempos y formas fundamentales: clasificación *O, O*.

Infinitivo

I will try *to* wake eərlier tomorrow.
(Trataré de despertar más temprano mañana.)

Presente

(af.)   Paul wakes early *every morning*.
(Pablo se despierta temprano todas las mañanas.)

(neg.)   Paul DOES NOT wake early *every morning*.

(int.)   DOES Paul wake early *every morning?*

Pasado

(af.)   You w*O*ke me very late *yesterday morning*.
(Usted me despertó muy tarde ayer en la mañana.)

(neg.)   You DID NOT *wake* me very late *yesterday morning*.

(int.)   DID you *wake* me very late *yesterday morning?*

Antepresente

(af.)   They *have* w*O*ke early because of the alarm clock.
(Ellos se han despertado temprano debido al reloj despertador.)

(neg.)   They *have* NOT w*O*ke early because of the alarm clock.

(int.)   *Have* they w*O*ke early because of the alarm clock?

Clasificación: *A, A.*

Características: Observe que estos tres verbos irregulares tienen en común la vocal *a* en sus pasado y participio pasado. Sus infinitivos son distintos.

Dicha vocal *a* posee un sonido intermedio entre la *a* y la *e (a/e)* en *sat* y *have.* En cambio se pronuncia *ei* en *make* y *made.* Las *e* finales son mudas.

Infinitivo	Pasado	Participio Pasado
1. *to* sit (sentarse)	sAt (se sentó)	sAt (sentado)
2. *to* have (tener, haber)	hAd (tuvo, hubo)	hAd (tenido, habido)
3. *to* make (hacer, manufacturar)	mAde (hizo, manufacturó)	mAde (hecho, manufacturado)

Ejemplos ilustrativos de cómo emplear el verbo marcado con el número 1 en sus tiempos y formas fundamentales: clasificación *A, A.*

Infinitivo

My grandfather likes *to* sit in his easy-chair.
(A mi abuelo le gusta sentarse en su sofá.)

Presente

(af.)   They sit in the park *every Sunday.*
(Ellos se sientan en el parque todos los domingos.)

(neg.) They DO NOT sit in the park *every Sunday.*

(int.) DO they sit in the park *every Sunday?*

Pasado

(af.)   John sAt in the waiting-room for a long time *yesterday.*
(Juan se sentó en la sala de espera mucho tiempo ayer.)

(neg.) John DID NOT *sit* in the waiting-room for a long time *yesterday.*

(int.) DID John *sit* in the waiting-room for a long time *yesterday?*

Antepresente

(af.) They *have* s*A*t on that bench many times.
(Ellos se han sentado en ese banco muchas veces.)

(neg.) They *have* NOT s*A*t on that bench many times.

(int.) *Have* they s*A*t on that bench many times?

Ejemplos ilustrativos de cómo emplear el verbo marcado con el número 2 en sus tiempos y formas fundamentales: clasificación *A, A.*

Infinitivo

We are going *to* have another child soon.
(Vamos a tener otro niño pronto.)

Presente

(af.) Robert has a house in the country.
(Roberto tiene una casa en el campo.)

(neg.) Robert DOES NOT have a house in the country.

(int.) DOES Robert have a house in the country?

Pasado

(af.) That man h*A*d a ranch *many years ago.*
(Ese hombre tuvo un rancho hace muchos años.)

(neg.) That man DID NOT *have* a ranch *many years ago.*

(int.) DID that man *have* a ranch *many years ago?*

Antepresente

(af.) They *have* h*A*d too much work *lately.*
(Ellos han tenido demasiado trabajo últimamente.)

(neg.) They *have* NOT h*A*d too much work *lately.*

(int.) *Have* they h*A*d too much work *lately?*

Ejemplos ilustrativos de cómo emplear el verbo marcado con el número 3 en sus tiempos y formas fundamentales: clasificación *A, A.*

Infinitivo

That country plans *to* make faster airplanes.
(Ese país proyecta hacer aviones más rápidos.)

Presente

(af.)   They make good furniture.
(Ellos hacen buenos muebles.)

(neg.) They DO NOT make good furniture.

(int.) DO they make good furniture?

Pasado

(af.)   Henry m*A*de many mistakes *yesterday.*
(Enrique hizo muchos errores ayer.)

(neg.) Henry DID NOT *make* many mistakes *yesterday.*

(int.) DID Henry *make* many mistakes *yesterday?*

Antepresente

(af.)   That carpenter *has* m*A*de many tables and chairs.
(Ese carpintero ha hecho muchas mesas y sillas.)

(neg.) That carpenter *has* NOT m*A*de many tables and chairs.

(int.) *Has* that carpenter m*A*de many tables and chairs?

SEGUNDO GRUPO

VERBOS CON FORMAS DISTINTAS EN EL INFINITIVO, PASADO Y PARTICIPIO PASADO

Clasificación: *IN, AN, UN.*

Características: El rasgo común en los infinitivos es la combinación *in*, en el pasado la *an* y en el participio pasado la *un* (excepto en *swim, swam, swum,* que consta de *m* en lugar de *n).*

Fonética: Pronúnciese la *i* con la abertura de la *e* castellana, pero tratando de emitir el sonido de la *i* latina, logrando así un sonido entre la *i* y la *e (a/e)* y la *u* con sonido equivalente a la *o* española.

Infinitivo	Pasado	Participio Pasado
IN	AN	UN
1. *to* beg*IN* (empezar)	beg*AN* (empezó)	beg*UN* (empezado)
2. *to* dr*IN*k (beber)	dr*AN*k (bebió)	dr*UN*k (bebido)
3. *to* s*IN*k (hundirse)	s*AN*k (se hundió)	s*UN*k (hundido)
4. *to* st*IN*k (apestar)	st*AN*k (apestó)	st*UN*k (apestado)
5. *to* shr*IN*k (encogerse)	shr*AN*k (se encogió)	shr*UN*k (encogido)
6. *to* sw*IM* (nadar)	sw*AM* (nadó)	sw*UM* (nadado)
7. *to* s*IN*g (cantar)	s*AN*g (contó)	s*UN*g (cantado)
8. *to* r*IN*g (sonar, tocar)	r*AN*g (sonó, tocó)	r*UN*g (sonado, tocado)
9. *to* run (correr)	r*AN* (corrió)	r*UN* (corrido)

Nota: To begin, to swim, y to run duplican su consonante final en el gerundio: begin*N*ing, swim*M*ing, run*N*ing.

Ejemplos ilustrativos de cómo emplear el verbo marcado con el número 1 en sus tiempos y formas fundamentales: clasificación *IN, AN, UN*.

Infinitivo

I have *to* beg*IN* this assignment as soon as possible.
(Tengo que empezar este trabajo tan pronto como sea posible.)

Presente

(af.) The teacher beg*IN*s the clase early *every day*.
(El maestro empieza la clase temprano todos los días.)

(neg.) The teacher DOES NOT beg*IN* the class early *every day*.

(int.) DOES the teacher beg*IN* the class early *every day?*

Pasado

(af.) The teacher beg*AN* the class very late *yesterday*.
(El maestro empezó la clase muy tarde ayer.)

(neg.) The teacher DID NOT beg*in* the class very late *yesterday*.

(int.) DID the teacher beg*in* the class very late *yesterday?*

Antepresente

(af.) Robert *has* beg*UN* an intensive training.
(Roberto ha empezado un entrenamiento intensivo.)

(neg.) Robert *has* NOT beg*UN* an intensive training.

(int.) *Has* Robert beg*UN* an intensive training?

Ejemplos ilustrativos de cómo emplear el verbo marcado con el número 2 en sus tiempos y formas fundamentales: clasificación *IN, AN, UN*.

Infinitivo

I like *to* dr*IN*k coffee in the morning.
(Me gusta tomar café en la mañana.)

Presente

(af.)   Paul dr*IN*ks coffee in the morning.
        (Pablo toma café en la mañana.)

(neg.)   Paul DOES NOT dr*IN*k coffee in the morning.

(int.)   DOES Paul dr*IN*k coffee in the morning?

Pasado

(af.)   Paul dr*AN*k coffee *yesterday morning*.
        (Pablo tomó café ayer en la mañana.)

(neg.)   Paul DID NOT drink coffee *yesterday morning*.

(int.)   DID Paul drink cofee *yesterday morning?*

Antepresente

(af.)   Paul *has* dr*UN*k too much coffee.
        (Pablo ha tomado demasiado café.)

(neg.)   Paul *has* NOT dr*UN*k too much coffee.

(int.)   *Has* Paul dr*UN*k too much coffee?

Ejemplos ilustrativos de cómo emplear el verbo marcado con el número 3 en sus tiempos y formas fundamentales: clasificación *IN, AN, UN*.

Infinitivo

That ship is not going *to* s*IN*k in spite of the storm.
(Ese barco no se va a hundir a pesar de la tormenta.)

Presente

(af.)   I s*IN*k in the water when I swim.
        (Me hundo en el agua cuando nado.)

(neg.)   I DO NOT s*IN*k in the water when I swim.

(int.)   DO I s*IN*k in the water when I swim?

Pasado

(af.)   I s*AN*k in the water when I was swimming *yesterday*.
        (Me hundí en el agua cuando estuve nadando ayer.)

(neg.) I DID NOT sink in the water when I was swimming *yesterday*.

(int.) DID I sink in the water when I was swimming *yesterday?*

Antepresente

(af.) The enemy *has* sUNk many ships.
(El enemigo ha hundido muchos barcos.)

(neg.) The enemy *has* NOT sUNk many ships.

(int.) *Has* the enemy sUNk many ships?

Ejemplos ilustrativos de cómo emplear el verbo marcado con el número 4 en sus tiempos y formas fundamentales: clasificación *IN, AN, UN*.

Infinitivo

That thing does not have *to* stINk at all.
(Esa cosa no tiene que apestar en lo absoluto.)

Presente

(af.) It stINks when it is not clean.
(Apesta cuando no está limpio.)

(neg.) It DOES NOT stINk when it is clean.

(int.) DOES it stINk when it is clean?

Pasado

(af.) It stANk because it was not clean.
(Apestó porque no estaba limpio.)

(neg.) It DID NOT stink because it was clean.
(No apestó porque estaba limpio.)

(int.) DID it stink because it was not clean?

Antepresente

(af.) That fish *has* stUNk because it is not fresh.
(Ese pescado ha apestado porque no está fresco.)

(neg.)   That fish *has* NOT st*UN*k because it is fresh.
(Ese pescado no ha apestado porque está fresco.)

(int.)   *Has* that fish st*UN*k because it is not fresh?

Ejemplos ilustrativos de cómo emplear el verbo marcado con el número 5 en sus tiempos y formas fundamentales: clasificación *IN, AN, UN.*

Infinitivo

This shirt is going *to* shr*IN*k when washed.
(Esta camisa se va a encoger cuando se lave.)

Presente

(af.)   These clothes* shr*IN*k when washed.
(Esta ropa se encoge cuando se lava.)

(neg.)   These clothes* DO NOT shr*IN*k when washed.

(int.)   DO these clothes* shr*IN*k when washed?

Pasado

(af.)   This shirt shr*AN*k when washed.
(Esta camisa se encogió cuando se lavó.)

(neg.)   This shirt DID NOT shr*in*k when washed.

(int.)   DID this shirt shr*in*k when washed?

Antepresente

(af.)   Those clothes* *have* shr*UN*k when washed.
(Esa ropa ha encogido cuando se lavó.)

(neg.)   Those clothes* *have* NOT shr*UN*k when washed.

(int.)   *Have* those clothes* shr*UN*k when washed?

* *Clothes* (ropa) es plural en inglés.

104

Ejemplos ilustrativos de cómo emplear el verbo marcado con el número 6 en sus tiempos y formas fundamentales: clasificación *IN, AN, UN.*

Infinitivo

We like *to* sw*I*M in the swimming-pool.
(Nos gusta nadar en la piscina de natación.)

Presente

(af.)   The students sw*I*M in the pool *every Sunday.*
(Los estudiantes nadan en la piscina todos los domingos.)

(neg.)   The students DO NOT sw*I*M in the pool *every Sunday.*

(int.)   DO the students sw*I*M in the pool *every Sunday?*

Pasado

(af.)   Robert sw*A*M in the lake *yesterday.*
(Roberto nadó en el lago ayer.)

(neg.)   Robert DID NOT sw*im* in the lake *yesterday.*

(int.)   DID Robert sw*im* in the lake *yesterday?*

Antepresente

(af.)   The boys *have* sw*U*M in the river *many times.*
(Los muchachos han nadado en el río muchas veces.)

(neg.)   The boys *have* NOT sw*U*M in the river *many times.*

(int.)   *Have* the boys sw*U*M in the river *many times?*

Ejemplos ilustrativos de cómo emplear el verbo marcado con el número 7 en sus tiempos y formas fundamentales: clasificación *IN, AN, UN.*

Infinitivo

The students are going *to* s*I*Ng in the school choir.
(Los estudiantes van a cantar en el coro de la escuela.)

(af.) Those singers s*IN*g on television *every week*.
(Esos cantantes cantan por televisión cada semana.)

(neg.) Those singers DO NOT s*IN*g on television *every week*.

(int.) DO those singers s*IN*g on television *every week?*

Pasado

(af.) Mary s*AN*g in the party *yesterday*.
(María cantó en la fiesta ayer.)

(neg.) Mary DID NOT sing in the party *yesterday*.

(int.) DID Mary sing in the party *yesterday?*

Antepresente

(af.) That singer *has* s*UN*g on television *many times*.
(Ese cantante ha cantado por televisión muchas veces.)

(neg.) That singer *has* NOT s*UN*g on television *many times*.

(int.) *Has* that singer s*UN*g on television *many times?*

Ejemplos ilustrativos de cómo emplear el verbo marcado con el número 8 en sus tiempos y formas fundamentales: clasificación *IN, AN, UN.*

Infinitivo

He is going *to* r*IN*g the church-bell.
(Él va a tocar la campana de la iglesia.)

Presente

(af.) George r*IN*gs the door-bell before he enters his house.
(Jorge toca el timbre de la puerta antes de entrar a su casa.)

(neg.) George DOES NOT r*IN*g the door-bell before he enters his house.

(int.) DOES George r*IN*g the door-bell before ore he enters his house?

Pasado

(af.) The telephone r*AN*g many times *yesterday*.
(El teléfono sonó muchas veces ayer.)

(neg.) The telephone DID NOT ring many times *yesterday*.

(int.) DID the telephone ring many times *yesterday?*

Antepresente

(af.) The telephone *has* r*UN*g many times *today*.
(El teléfono ha sonado muchas veces hoy.)

(neg.) The telephone *has* NOT r*UN*g many times *today*.

(int.) *Has* the telephone r*UN*g many times *today?*

Ejemplos ilustrativos de cómo emplear el verbo marcado con el número 9 en sus tiempos y formas fundamentales: clasificación *IN, AN, UN*.

Infinitivo

John likes *to* r*UN* in the park.
(A Juan le gusta correr en el parque.)

Presente

(af.) The boys *run* in the yard *every day*.
(Los muchachos corren en el patio todos los días.)

(neg.) The boys DO NOT *run* in the yard *every day*.

(int.) DO the boys *run* in the yard *every day?*

Pasado

(af.) Charles r*AN* to school *yesterday*.
(Carlos corrió a la escuela ayer.)

(neg.) Charles DID NOT *run* to school *yesterday*.

(int.) DID Charles *run* to school *yesterday?*

Antepresente

(af.)   Henry *has* r*UN* many kilometers *lately*.
(Enrique ha corrido muchos kilómetros últimamente.)

(neg.) Henry *has* NOT r*UN* many kilometers *lately*.

(int.) *Has* Henry r*UN* many kilometers *lately*?

NOTA: Obsérvese que la forma simple de to run es idéntica a su participio pasado: run-corrido.

Clasificación: *I-E, O-E, I-EN*.

Características: En este grupo el rasgo característico del infinitivo son las vocales separadas *(i-e)*, en el pasado *(o-e)* y en el participio pasado *(i-en)*. El guión (-) que se interpone entre las vocales significa que existe una consonante entre ellas (to dri*ve*, dro*ve*, dri*ven*). En algunos participios pasados existe la doble consonante idéntica interponiéndose entre *i-en* como en wri*tten*, ri*dden*, etcétera.

Fonética: En el infinitivo la vocal *i* tiene sonido equivalente en español de *ai*, mientras que en el participio pasado suena igual que en castellano. La *e* final es muda en el infinitivo y el pasado.

Infinitivo	*Pasado*	*Participio Pasado*
I-E	*O-E*	*I-EN*
1. *to* wr*I*tt*E* (escribir)	wr*O*t*E* (escribió)	wr*I*tt*EN* (escrito)
2. *to* dr*I*v*E* (manejar)	dr*O*v*E* (manejó)	dr*I*v*EN* (manejado)
3. *to* r*I*d*E* (montar, viajar en vehículo)	r*O*d*E* (montó, viajó)	r*I*dd*EN* (montado, viajado)
4. *to* r*I*s*E* (levantarse)	r*O*s*E* (se levantó)	r*I*s*EN* (levantado)
5. *to* str*I*v*E* (esforzarse)	str*O*v*E* (se esforzó)	str*I*v*EN* (esforzado)
6. *to* str*I*d*E* (caminar a grandes pasos)	str*O*d*E* (caminó)	str*I*dd*EN* (caminado)

Ejemplos ilustrativos de cómo emplear el verbo marcado con el número 1 en sus tiempos y formas fundamentales: clasificación *I-E, O-E, I-EN*.

Infinitivo

I have *to* wr*I*t*E* a report on sales.
(**Tengo** que escribir un informe sobre ventas.)

Presente

(af.)   The secretary wr*It*Es many letters *every day*.
(La secretaria escribe muchas cartas todos los días.)

(neg.) The secretary DOES NOT wr*It*E many letters *every day*.

(int.) DOES the secretary wr*It*E many letters *every day?*

Pasado

(af.)   Helen wr*OtE* a letter to her parents *yesterday*.
(Elena escribió una carta a sus padres ayer.)

(neg.) Helen DID NOT write a letter to her parents *yesterday*.

(int.) DID Helen write a letter to her parents *yesterday?*

Antepresente

(af.)   The employees *have* wr*Itt*EN a long report.
(Los empleados han escrito un largo informe.)

(neg.) The employees *have* NOT wr*Itt*EN a long report.

(int.) *Have* the employees wr*Itt*EN a long report?

Ejemplos ilustrativos de cómo emplear el verbo marcado con el número 2 en sus tiempos y formas fundamentales: clasificación *I-E, O-E, I-EN*.

Infinitivo

We are going *to* dr*Iv*E from New York to Chicago.
(Vamos a manejar de Nueva York a Chicago.)

Presente

(af.)   They dr*Iv*E carefully at night.
(Ellos manejan con cuidado en la noche.)

(neg.) They DO NOT dr*Iv*E carefully at night.

(int.) DO they dr*Iv*E carefully at night?

Pasado

(af.) You drOvE the car very fast *last night.*
(Tú manejaste el auto muy rápido anoche.)

(neg.) You DID NOT drive the car very fast *last night.*

(int.) DID you drive the car very fast *last night?*

Antepresente

(af.) Albert *has* drIvEN that truck *many times.*
(Alberto ha manejado ese camión muchas veces.)

(neg.) Albert *has* NOT drIvEN that truck *many times.*

(int.) *Has* Albert drIvEN that truck *many times?*

Ejemplos ilustrativos de cómo emplear el verbo marcado con el número 3 en sus tiempos y formas fundamentales: clasificación *I-E, O-E, I-EN.*

Infinitivo

(Paul likes *to* rIdE on a horse.
(A Pablo le gusta montar a caballo.)

Presente

(af.) The woman rIdEs in the bus *every day.*
(La mujer viaja en autobús todos los días.)

(neg.) The woman DOES NOT rIdE in the bus *every day.*

(int.) DOES the woman rIdE in the bus *every day?*

Pasado

(af.) My cousin rOdE on his motorcycle *yesterday.*
(Mi primo montó en su motocicleta ayer.)

(neg.) My cousin DID NOT ride on his motorcycle *yesterday.*

(int.) DID my cousin ride on his motorcycle *yesterday?*

Antepresente

(af.) My uncle *has* rIddEN on a train *many times.*
(Mi tío ha viajado en tren muchas veces.)

(neg.)   My uncle *has* NOT r*Idd*EN on a train *many times.*

(int.)   *Has* my uncle r*Idd*EN on a train *many times?*

Ejemplos ilustrativos de cómo emplear el verbo marcado con el número 4 en sus tiempos y formas fundamentales: clasificación *I-E, O-E, I-EN.*

Infinitivo

I like *to* r*Is*E early in the morning.
(Me gusta levantarme temprano en la mañana.)

Presente

(af.)   We r*Is*E early *every day.*
(Nos levantamos temprano todos los días.)

(neg.)   We DO NOT r*Is*E early *every day.*

(int.)   Do we r*Is*E early *every day?*

Pasado

(af.)   Henry r*Os*E very early *yesterday.*
(Enrique se levantó muy temprano ayer.)

(neg.)   Henry DID NOT r*ise* very early *yesterday.*

(int.)   DID Henry r*ise* very early *yesterday?*

Antepresente

(af.)   They *have* r*Is*EN early *all this week.*
(Ellos se han levantado temprano toda esta semana.)

(neg.)   They *have* NOT r*Is*EN early *all this week.*

(int.)   *Have* they r*Is*EN early *all this week?*

Ejemplos ilustrativos de cómo emplear el verbo marcado con el número 5 en sus tiempos y formas fundamentales: clasificación *I-E, O-E, I-EN.*

You have *to* str*Iv*E to learn more English.
(Tienes que esforzarte a aprender más inglés.)

112

Presente

(af.) The students str*Iv*E to learn more.
(Los estudiantes se esfuerzan por aprender más.)

(neg.) The students DO NOT str*Iv*E to learn more.

(int.) DO the students str*Iv*E to learn more?

Pasado

(af.) Mary str*Ov*E to earn a scholarship *last year*.
(María se esforzó por ganar una beca el año pasado.)

(neg.) Mary DID NOT strive to earn a scholarship *last year*.

(int.) DID Mary strive to earn a scholarship *last year?*

Antepresente

(af.) They *have* str*Iv*EN to be good students.
(Ellos se han esforzado en ser buenos estudiantes.)

(neg.) They *have* NOT str*Iv*EN to be good students.

(int.) *Have* they str*Iv*EN to be good students?

Ejemplos ilustrativos de cómo emplear el verbo marcado con el número 6 en sus tiempos y formas fundamentales: clasificación *I-E, O-E, I-EN.*

Infinitivo

Mr. Davies likes *to* str*Id*E out of his office.
(Al señor Davies le gusta salir a grandes pasos de su despacho.)

Presente

(af.) John str*Id*Es to school *every day*.
(Juan camina a grandes pasos a la escuela todos los días.)

(neg.) John DOES NOT str*Id*E to school *every day*.

(int.) DOES John str*Id*E to school *every day?*

Pasado

(af.) Paul str*Od*E into the room *yesterday*.
(Pablo entró a grandes pasos al cuarto ayer.)

(neg.) Paul DID NOT stride into the room *yesterday*.

(int.) DID Paul stride into the room *yesterday?*

Antepresente

(af.) The students *have* str*I*dd*EN* to school very *often*.
(Los estudiantes han caminado a grandes pasos a la escuela muy a menudo.)

(neg.) The students *have* NOT str*I*dd*EN* to school very *often*.

(int.) *Have* the students str*I*dd*EN* to school very *often*.

Clasificación: *E-A, O-E, O-EN.*

Características: Vocales comunes en el infinitivo *ea;* en el pasado *o-e* y en el participio pasado *o-en.* Observe que to ch*oo*se y to fr*ee*ze tienen características desafines a los demás sólo en el infinitivo.

Fonética: En este grupo la combinación *ea* tiene sonido de *i* latina; tanto en el pasado como en el participio pasado la vocal *o* se pronuncia *ou.* La *e* final es muda en el pasado. Pronúnciese la *ee* de fr*ee*ze como *i* latina y la *oo* de ch*oo*se con sonido de *u.* La *ea* de to br*ea*k suena *ei.*

Infinitivo	*Pasado*	*Participio Pasado*
EA	*O-E*	*O-EN*
1. *to* sp*EA*k (hablar)	sp*Ok*E (habló)	sp*Ok*E*N* (hablado)
2. to st*EA*l (robar)	st*Ol*E (robó)	st*Ol*E*N* (robado)
2. *to* br*EA*k (romper)	br*Ok*E (rompió)	br*Ok*E*N* (roto)
4. *to* w*EA*ve (hilar, entrelazar)	w*Ov*E (hiló, entrelazó)	w*Ov*E*N* (hilado, entrelazado)
5. *to* ch*OO*se (escoger)	ch*Os*E (escogió)	ch*Os*E*N* (escogido)
6. *to* fr*EE*ze (congelar)	fr*Oz*E (congeló)	fr*Oz*E*N* (congelado)

Ejemplos ilustrativos de cómo emplear el verbo marcado con el número 1 en sus tiempos y formas fundamentales: clasificación *E-A, O-E, O-EN.*

Infinitivo

My brother likes *to* sp*EA*k English all the time.
(A mi hermano le gusta hablar inglés todo el tiempo.)

(af.) He sp*EA*ks to them in English *every day.*
(Él les habla en inglés todos los días.)

(neg.) He DOES NOT sp*EA*k to them in English *every day.*

(int.) DOES he sp*EA*k to them in English *every day?*

Pasado

(af.) The manager sp*OkE* in the meeting *yesterday.*
(El gerente habló en la junta ayer.)

(neg.) The manager DID NOT sp*eak* in the meeting *yesterday.*

(int.) DID the manager sp*eak* in the meeting *yesterday?*

Antepresente

(af.) They *have* sp*OkEN* English during the meeting.
(Ellos han hablado inglés durante la junta.)

(neg.) They *have* NOT sp*OkEN* English during the meeting.

(int.) *Have* they sp*OkEN* English during the meeting?

Ejemplos ilustrativos de cómo emplear el verbo marcado con el número 2 en sus tiempos y formas fundamentales: clasificación *E-A, O-E, O-EN.*

Infinitivo

Peter does not like *to* st*EA*l money.
(A Pedro no le gusta robar dinero.)

Presente

(af.) That boy st*EA*ls things from his friends.
(Ese muchacho roba cosas a sus amigos.)

(neg.) That boy DOES NOT st*EA*l things from his friends.

(int.) DOES that boy st*EA*l things from his friends?

Pasado

(af.) He st*OlE* money from the bank.
(Él robó dinero del banco.)

116

(neg.) He DID NOT steal money from the bank.

(int.) DID he steal money from the bank?

Antepresente

(af.) That player *has* st*O1EN* many bases in the base-ball game.
(Ese jugador ha robado muchas bases en el juego de beisbol.)

(neg.) That player *has* NOT st*O1EN* many bases in the base-ball game.

(int.) *Has* that player st*O1EN* many bases in the base-ball game?

Ejemplos ilustrativos de cómo emplear el verbo marcado con el número 3 en sus tiempos y formas fundamentales: clasificación *E-A, O-E, O-EN.*

Infinitivo

Mexico is not going *to* br*EA*k relations with that country.
(México no va a romper relaciones con ese país.)

Presente

(af.) Richard br*EA*ks his friends' toys.
(Ricardo rompe los juguetes de sus amigos.)

(neg.) Richards DOES NOT br*EA*k his friends' toys.

(int.) DOES Richard br*EA*k his friends' toys?

Pasado

(af.) Paul br*OkE* his arm *last week.*
(Pablo se rompió el brazo la semana pasada.)

(neg.) Paul DID NOT break his arm *last week.*

(int.) DID Paul break his arm *last week?*

Antepresente

(af.) He *has* br*OkEN* the law *many times.*
(Él ha quebrantado la ley muchas veces.)

(neg.) He *has* NOT br*OkEN* the law *many times.*

(int.) *Has* he br*OkEN* the law *many times?*

Ejemplos ilustrativos de cómo emplear el verbo marcado con el número 4 en sus tiempos y formas fundamentales: clasificación *E-A, O-E, O-EN*.

Infinitivo

Mary is learning *to* w*EA*ve.
(María está aprendiendo a hilar.)

Presente

(af.)   That girl w*EA*ves beautiful cloth.
(Esa muchacha hila hermosa tela.)

(neg.)   That girl DOES NOT w*EA*ve beautiful cloth.

(int.)   DOES that girl w*EA*ve beautiful cloth?

Pasado

(af.)   She w*OvE* this cloth *last year.*)
(Ella hiló esta tela el año pasado.)

(neg.)   She DID NOT w*eave* this cloth *last year.*

(int.)   DID she w*eave* this cloth *last year?*

Antepresente

(af.)   That woman *has* w*OvEN* cloth *before.*
(Esa mujer ha hilado tela antes.)

(neg.)   That woman *has* NOT w*OvEN* cloth *before.*

(int.)   *Has* that woman w*OvEN* cloth *before?*

Ejemplos ilustrativos de cómo emplear el verbo marcado con el número 5 en sus tiempos y formas fundamentales: clasificación *E-A, O-E, O-EN*.

Infinitivo

I am trying *to* ch*OO*se a nice color.
(Estoy tratando de escoger un bonito color.)

Presente

(af.) Mrs. Miller chOOses the neckties for her husband.
(La señora Miller escoge las corbatas para su esposo.)

(neg.) Mrs. Miller DOES NOT chOOse the neckties for her husband.

(int.) DOES Mrs. Miller chOOse the neckties for her husband?

Pasado

(af.) Mother chOsE the curtains for the living room.
(Mamá escogió las cortinas para la estancia.)

(neg.) Mother DID NOT choose the curtains for the living room.

(int.) DID mother choose the curtains for the living room?

Antepresente

(af.) The boys *have* chOsEN John for president.
(Los muchachos han escogido a Juan para presidente.)

(neg.) The boys *have* NOT chOsEN John for president.

(int.) *Have* the boys chOsEN John for president?

Ejemplos ilustrativos de cómo emplear el verbo marcado con el número 6 en sus tiempos y formas fundamentales: clasificación *E-A, O-E, O-EN*.

Infinitivo

That food is probably going *to* frEEze in the ice-box.
(Esta comida probablemente se va a congelar en la nevera.)

Presente

(af.) This refrigerator frEEzes the ice-cubes very fast.
(Este refrigerador congela los cubitos de hielo muy rápido.)

(neg.) This refrigerator DOES NOT frEEze the ice-cubes very fast.

(int.) DOES this refrigerator frEEze the ice-cubes very fast?

119

Pasado

(af.) The snow fr*Oz*E the crops *last Winter*.
(La nieve congeló las cosechas el invierno pasado.)

(neg.) The snow DID NOT freeze the crops *last Winter*.

(int.) DID the snow freeze the crops *last Winter?*

Antepresente

(af.) The cold-wave *has* fr*OzEN* the plants *this Winter*.
(La onda fría ha congelado las plantas este invierno.)

(neg.) The cold-wave *has* NOT fr*OzEN* the plants *this Winter*.

(int.) *Has* the cold-wave fr*OzEN* the plants *this Winter?*

Clasificación: *OW, EW, OWN.*

Características: Observe la combinación *ow* como rasgo afín en el infinitivo; *ew* en el pasado y *own* en el participio pasado.

Fonética: *Ow* suena *ou; ew* como *u* excepto en kn*ew* que suena *iú* y *own* como *óun.* En *fly* la *y* se pronuncia *ai.*

Infinitivo OW (ou)	Pasado EW (u)	Participio Pasado OWN (óun)
1. *to* kn*OW* (saber, conocer)	kn*EW* (supo, conoció)	kn*OWN* (sabido, conocido)
2. *to* gr*OW* (crecer, cultivar)	gr*EW* (creció, cultivó)	gr*OWN* (crecido, cultivado)
3. *to* thr*OW* (arrojar, lanzar)	thr*EW* (arrojó, lanzó)	thr*OWN* (arrojado, lanzado)
4. *to* bl*OW* (soplar, sonarse la nariz)	bl*EW* (sopló, se sonó la nariz)	bl*OWN* (soplado, sonado la nariz)
5. *to* fly (volar)	fl*EW* (voló)	fl*OWN* (volado)

Sub-clasificación: *AW, EW, AWN.*

Características: Infinitivo *aw,* pasado *ew* y participio pasado *awn.*

Fonética: *aw* tiene sonido de *o; ew* se pronuncia *u* y *awn* como *on.*

Infinitivo AW (o)	Pasado EW (u)	Participio Pasado AWN (on)
1. *to* dr*AW* (dibujar, sacar)	dr*EW* (dibujó, sacó)	dr*AWN* (dibujado, sacado)
2. *to* withdr*AW* (retirar)	withdr*EW* (retiró)	withdr*AWN* (retirado)
3. *to* overdr*AW* (sobregirar)	overdr*EW* (sobregiró)	overdr*AWN* (sobregirado)

Ejemplos ilustrativos de cómo emplear el verbo marcado con el número 1 en sus tiempos y formas fundamentales: clasificación *OW, EW, OWN*.

Infinitivo

I would like *to* kn*OW* more about that matter.
(Me gustaría saber más acerca de ese asunto.)

Presente

(af.)   They kn*OW* everything about sales promotion.
(Ellos saben todo respecto a promoción de ventas.)

(neg.)   They DO NOT kn*OW* everything about sales promotion.

(int.)   DO they kn*OW* everything about sales promotion?

Pasado

(af.)   My grandfather kn*EW* London *many years ago*.
(Mi abuelo conoció Londres hace muchos años.)

(neg.)   My grandfather DID NOT kn*ow* London.

(int.)   DID my grandfather kn*ow* London *many years ago?*

Antepresente

(af.)   We *have* kn*OWN* many things about New York.
(Hemos sabido muchas cosas acerca de Nueva York.)

(neg.)   We *have* NOT kn*OWN* many things about New York.

(int.)   *Have* we kn*OWN* many things about New York?

Ejemplos ilustrativos de cómo emplear el verbo marcado con el número 2 en sus tiempos y formas fundamentales: clasificación *OW, EW, OWN*.

Infinitivo

He is going *to* gr*OW* as tall as his father.
(Él va a crecer tan alto como su padre.)

Presente

(af.) Those farmers gr*OW* cotton in the farm.
(Esos granjeros cultivan algodón en la granja.)

(neg.) Those farmers DO NOT gr*OW* cotton in the farm.

(int.) DO those farmers gr*OW* cotton in the farm?

Pasado

(af.) Mary gr*EW* as tall as her mother.
(María creció tan alta como su madre.)

(neg.) Mary DID NOT grow as tall as her mother.

(int.) DID Mary grow as tall as her mother?

Antepresente

(af.) He *has* gr*OWN* many roses in his garden.
(Él ha cultivado muchas rosas en su jardín.)

(neg.) He *has* NOT gr*OWN* many roses in his garden.

(int.) *Has* he gr*OWN* many roses in his garden?

Ejemplos ilustrativos de cómo emplear el verbo marcado con el número 3 en sus tiempos y formas fundamentales: clasificación *OW*, *EW*, *OWN*.

Infinitivo

Peter likes *to* thr*OW* snow-balls to his friends.
(A Pedro le gusta arrojar bolas de nieve a sus amigos.)

Presente

(af.) Richard thr*OW*s the ball very high.
(Ricardo lanza la pelota muy alto.)

(neg.) Richard DOES NOT thr*OW* the ball very high.

(int.) DOES Richard thr*OW* the ball very high?

Pasado

(af.) That boy thr*EW* a stone against the door.
(Ese muchacho arrojó una piedra contra la puerta.)

(neg.)   That boy DID NOT thr*ow* a stone against the door.

(int.)   DID that boy thr*ow* a stone against the door?

Antepresente

(af.)   He *has* thr*OWN* the garbage on the floor.
(Él ha tirado la basura en el piso.)

(neg.)   He *has* NOT thr*OWN* the garbage on the floor.

(int.)   *Has* he thr*OWN* the garbage on the floor?

Ejemplos ilustrativos de cómo emplear el verbo marcado con el número 4 en sus tiempos y formas fundamentales: clasificación *OW, EW, OWN*.

Infinitivo

The wind is going *to* bl*OW* in the mountains.
(El viento va a soplar en las montañas.)

Presente

(af.)   I bl*OW* my nose many times whenever I have a cold.
(Me sueno la nariz muchas veces cuando tengo catarro.)

(neg.)   I DO NOT bl*OW* my nose many times whenever I have a cold.

(int.)   DO I bl*OW* my nose many times whenever I have a cold?

Pasado

(af.)   The wind bl*EW* very hard *yesterday*.
(El viento sopló muy fuerte ayer.)

(neg.)   The wind DID NOT blow very hard *yesterday*.

(int.)   DID the wind blow very hard *yesterday?*

Antepresente

(af.)   John *has* bl*OWN* his nose *many times*.
(Juan se ha sonado la nariz muchas veces.)

(neg.)   John *has* NOT bl*OWN* his nose *many times*.

(int.)   *Has* John bl*OWN* his nose *many times?*

Ejemplos ilustrativos de cómo emplear el verbo marcado con el número 5 en sus tiempos y formas fundamentales: clasificación *OW, EW, OWN*.

Infinitivo

Mr. Brown likes *to* fly on jet planes.
(Al señor Brown le gusta volar en aviones de retropropulsión.)

Presente

(af.)   Some birds fly to warmer climates during *Winter*.
(Algunas aves vuelan a climas más cálidos durante el invierno.)

(neg.)   Some birds DO NOT fly to warmer climates during *Winter*.

(int.)   DO some birds fly to warmer climates during *Winter?*

Pasado

(af.)   Dr. Davies fl*EW* to New York *last week*.
(El doctor Davies voló a Nueva York la semana pasada.)

(neg.)   Dr. Davies DID NOT *fly* to New York *last week*.

(int.)   DID Dr. Davies *fly* to New York *last week?*

Antepresente

(af.)   My uncle *has* fl*OWN* on jet planes *many times*.
(Mi tío ha volado en aviones de propulsión muchas veces.)

(neg.)   My uncle *has* NOT fl*OWN* on jet planes *many times*.

(int.)   *Has* my uncle fl*OWN* on jet planes *many times?*

Ejemplos ilustrativos de cómo emplear el verbo marcado con el número 1 en sus tiempos y formas fundamentales: sub-clasificación *AW, EW, AWN*.

Infinitivo

Peter likes *to* dr*AW* pictures on the walls.
(A Pedro le gusta dibujar imágenes en las paredes.)

(af.)   They dr*AW* money *from* the bank *every month*.
        (Ellos sacan dinero del banco cada mes.)

(neg.) They DO NOT dr*AW* money *from* the bank *every month*.

(int.) DO they dr*AW* money *from* the bank *every month?*

Pasado

(af.)   They dr*EW* money *from* the bank *last month*.
        (Ellos sacaron dinero del banco el mes pasado.)

(neg.) They DID NOT dr*aw* money *from* the bank *last month*.

(int.) DID they dr*aw* money *from* the bank *last month?*

Antepresente

(af.)   The teacher *has* dr*AWN* many pictures on the black-board.
        (El maestro ha dibujado muchas imágenes en el pizarrón.)

(neg.) The teacher *has* NOT dr*AWN* many pictures on the blackboard.

(int.) *Has* the teacher dr*AWN* many pictures on the black-board?

Ejemplos ilustrativos de cómo emplear el verbo marcado con el número 2 en sus tiempos y formas fundamentales: subclasificación *AW, EW, AWN*.

Infinitivo

The general has *to* winthdr*AW* his troops from the battlefield.
(El general tiene que retirar sus tropas del campo de batalla.)

Presente

(af.)   The manager withdr*AW*s money from the bank *every month*.
        (El gerente retira dinero del banco todos los meses.)

(neg.) The manager DOES NOT withdr*AW* money from the bank *every month.*

(int.) DOES the manager withdr*AW* money from the bank *every month?*

Pasado

(af.) The soldiers withdr*EW* from the battlefield.
(Los soldados se retiraron del campo de batalla.)

(neg.) The soldiers DID NOT withdr*aw* from the battlefield.

(int.) DID the soldiers withdr*aw* from the battlefield?

Antepresente

(af.) My brother *has* dr*AWN* a lot of money from the bank *lately.*
(Mi hermano ha retirado mucho dinero del banco últimamente.)

(neg.) My brother *has* NOT dr*AWN* a lot of money from the bank *lately.*

(int.) *Has* my brother dr*AWN* a lot of money from the bank *lately?*

Ejemplos ilustrativos de cómo emplear el verbo marcado con el número 3 en sus tiempos y formas fundamentales: subclasificación *AW, EW, AWN.*

Infinitivo

He does not have *to* overdr*AW* in his bank account.
(Él no tiene que sobregirarse en su cuenta bancaria.)

Presente

(af.) I overdr*AW* in my expenses *every month.*
(Me sobregiro en mis gastos todos los meses.)

(neg.) I DO NOT overdr*AW* in my expenses *every month.*

(int.) DO I overdr*AW* in my expenses *every month?*

Pasado

(af.)   He overdr*EW* in his credit *last month*.
(Él se sobregiró en su crédito el mes pasado.)

(neg.)   He DID NOT overdr*aw* in his credit *last month*.

(int.)   DID he overdr*aw* in his credit *last month?*

Antepresente

(af.)   Mr. Brown *has* overdr*AWN* in his checks *lately*.
(El señor Brown se ha sobregirado en sus cheques últimamente.)

(neg.)   Mr. Brown *has* NOT overdr*AWN* in his checks *lately*.

(int.)   *Has* Mr. Brown overdr*AWN* in his checks *lately?*

Clasificación: *AKE, OOK, AKEN*.

Características: Letras afines en el infinitivo *ake*, en el pasado *ook* y en el participio pasado *aken*.

Fonética: *Ake* se pronuncia *éic*, *ook* tiene sonido de *uc* y *aken* como *éiken*. La *ú* de *to undertake* tiene sonido de *o*.

Infinitivo	Pasado	Participio Pasado
AKE (éic)	OOK (uc)	AKEN (éiken)
1. *to* t*AKE* (tomar, llevar)	t*OOK* (tomó, llevó)	t*AKEN* (tomado, llevado)
2. *to* mist*AKE* (confundir, equivocar)	mist*OOK* (confundió, equivocó)	mist*AKEN* (confundido, equivocado)
3. *to* undert*AKE* (emprender)	undert*OOK* (emprendió)	undert*AKEN* (emprendido)
4. *to* sh*AKE* (agitar, dar la mano)	sh*OOK* (agitó, dio la mano)	sh*AKEN* (agitado, dado la mano)
5. *to* fors*AKE* (abandonar)	fors*OOK* (abandonó)	fors*AKEN* (abandonado)

Ejemplos ilustrativos de cómo emplear el verbo marcado con el número 1 en sus tiempos y formas fundamentales: clasificación *AKE, OOK, AKEN*.

Infinitivo

Their father likes *to* t*AKE* them to the amusement park. (A su padre le gusta llevarlos al parque de diversión.)

Presente

(af.) The secretary t*AKE*s dictation *every day*. (La secretaria toma dictado todos los días.)

129

(neg.) The secretary DOES NOT t*AKE* dictation *every day*.

(int.) DOES the secretary t*AKE* dictation *every day?*

Pasado

(af.) John t*OOK* the boy to the circus *yesterday*.
(Juan llevó al niño al circo ayer.)

(neg.) John DID NOT t*ake* the boy to the circus *yesterday*.

(int.) DID John t*ake* the boy to the circus *yesterday?*

Antepresente

(af.) They *have* t*AKEN* an English course during this year.
(Ellos han tomado un curso de inglés durante este año.)

(neg.) They *have* NOT t*AKEN* an English course during this year.

(int.) *Have* they t*AKEN* an English course during this year?

Ejemplos ilustrativos de cómo emplear el verbo marcado con el número 2 en sus tiempos y formas fundamentales: clasificación *AKE, OOK, AKEN*.

Infinitivo

I DO NOT want *to* mist*AKE* you for another person.
(No quiero confundirte con otra persona.)

Presente

(af.) You mist*AKE* your calculations *frequently*.
(Te equivocas en tus calculos frecuentemente.)

(neg.) You DO NOT mist*AKE* your calculations *frequently*.

(int.) DO you mist*AKE* your calculations *frequently?*

Pasado

(af.) Mary mist*OOK* John for Charles *yesterday*.
(María confundió a Juan por Carlos ayer.)

(neg.) Mary DID NOT mist*ake* John for Charles *yesterday*.
(int.) DID Mary mist*ake* John for Charles *yesterday?*

Antepresente

(af.) I *have* mist*AKEN* my calculations.
(Me he equivocado en mis cálculos.)

(neg.) I *have* NOT mist*AKEN* my calculations.

(int.) *Have* I mist*AKEN* my calculations?

Ejemplos ilustrativos de cómo emplear el verbo marcado con el número 3 en sus tiempos y formas fundamentales: clasificación *AKE, OOK, AKEN.*

Infinitivo

He is going *to* undert*AKE* a long trip around the world.
(Él va a emprender un largo viaje alrededor del mundo.)

Presente

(af.) Those men undert*AKE* new activities *frequently.*
(Esos hombres emprenden nuevas actividades frecuentemente.)

(neg.) Those men DO NOT undert*AKE* new activities frequently.

(int.) DO those men undert*AKE* new activities *frequently?*

Pasado

(af.) John undert*OOK* an important task *last month.*
(Juan emprendió una tarea importante el mes pasado.)

(neg.) John DID NOT undert*AKE* an important task *last month.*

(int.) DID John undert*ake* an important task *last month?*

Antepresente

(af.) They *have* undert*AKEN* another rehabilitation plan.
(Ellos han emprendido otro plan de rehabilitación.)

(neg.) They *have* NOT undert*AKEN* another rehabilitation plan.

(int.) *Have* they undert*AKEN* another rehabilitation plan?

Ejemplos ilustrativos de cómo emplear el verbo marcado con el número 4 en sus tiempos y formas fundamentales: clasificación *AKE, OOK, AKEN*.

Infinitivo

I like *to* sh*AKE* hands with my friends.
(Me gusta dar la mano a mis amigos.)

Presente

(af.)   I sh*AKE* hands with my friends.
(Yo doy la mano a mis amigos.)

(neg.)   I DO NOT sh*AKE* hands with my friends.

(int.)   DO I sh*AKE* hands with my friends?

Pasado

(af.)   Robert sh*OOK* hands with us *last night*.
(Roberto nos dio la mano anoche.)

(neg.)   Robert DID NOT sh*ake* hands with us *last night*.

(int.)   DID Robert sh*ake* hands with us *last night?*

Antepresente

(af.)   The nurse *has* sh*AKEN* the medicine according to instructions.
(La enfermera ha agitado la medicina de acuerdo con las instrucciones.)

(neg.)   The nurse *has* ÑOT sh*AKEN* the medicine according to instructions.

(int.)   *Has* the nurse sh*AKEN* the medicine according to instructions?

Ejemplos ilustrativos de cómo emplear el verbo marcado con el número 5 en sus tiempos y formas fundamentales: clasificación *AKE, OOK, AKEN*.

Infinitivo

He is not going *to* fors*AKE* his relatives.
(Él no va a abandonar a sus familiares.)

Presente

(af.) They fors*AKE* their families when they grow up.
(Ellos abandonan a sus familias cuando crecen.)

(neg.) They DO NOT fors*AKE* their families when they grow up.

(int.) DO they fors*AKE* their families when they grow up?

Pasado

(af.) The tigress fors*OOK* her cubs when they grew up.
(La tigresa abandonó a sus cachorros cuando crecieron.)

(neg.) The tigress DID NOT fors*ake* her cubs when they grew up.

(int.) DID the tigress fors*ake* her cubs when they grew up?

Antepresente

(af.) He *has* fors*AKEN* them.
(Él los ha abandonado.)

(neg.) He *has* NOT fors*AKEN* them.

(int.) *Has* he fors*AKEN* them?

Clasificación: *EAR, ORE, ORN.*

Características: *Ear* es el rasgo afín en el infinitivo, *ore* en el pasado y *orn* en el participio pasado.

Fonética: Las letras afines en el infinitivo se pronuncian *er*, las del pasado *or* y las del participio pasado *orn*.

Infinitivo	Pasado	Participio Pasado
EAR (er)	ORE (or)	ORN (orn)
1. *to* w*EAR* (usar, llevar puesto)	w*ORE* (usó, llevó puesto)	w*ORN* (usado, llevado puesto)
2. *to* t*EAR* (desgarrar, arrancar)	t*ORE* (desgarró, arrancó)	t*ORN* (desgarrado, arrancado)
3. *to* sw*EAR* (jurar, blasfemar)	sw*ORE* (juró, blasfemó)	sw*ORN* (jurado, blasfemado)
4. *to* b*EAR* (parir, dar fruto, soportar)	b*ORE* (parió, dio fruto, soportó)	b*ORN* (parido, dado fruto, soportado)

Ejemplos ilustrativos de cómo emplear el verbo marcado con el número 1 en sus tiempos y formas fundamentales: clasificación *EAR, ORE, ORN.*

Infinitivo

Mary likes *to* w*EAR* beautiful dresses.
(A María le gusta usar vestidos hermosos.)

Presente

(af.) Some students w*EAR* a necktie in school.
(Algunos estudiantes usan corbata en la escuela.)

(neg.) Some students DO NOT w*EAR* a necktie in school.

(int.) DO some students w*EAR* a necktie in school?

134

(af.) Helen w*ORE* a blue dress in the party *last night*.
(Elena llevó puesto un vestido azul en la fiesta de anoche.)

(neg.) Helen DID NOT *wear* a blue dress in the party *last night*.

(int.) DID Helen *wear* a blue dress in the party *last night?*

Antepresente

(af.) Mrs. Taylor *has* w*ORN* her jewels *in every party*.
(La señora Taylor ha llevado puestas sus joyas en cada fiesta.)

(neg.) Mrs. Taylor *has* NOT w*ORN* her jewels *in every party*.

(int.) *Has* Mrs. Taylor w*ORN* her jewels *in every party?*

Ejemplos ilustrativos de cómo emplear el verbo marcado con el número 2 en sus tiempos y formas fundamentales: clasificación *EAR, ORE, ORN*.

Infinitivo

The dog was trying *to* t*EAR* his clothes.
(El perro estaba tratando de desgarrar su ropa.)

Presente

(af.) That little boy t*EAR*s his clothes when he is angry.
(Ese muchachito desgarra su ropa cuando se enoja.)

(neg.) That little boy DOES NOT t*EAR* his clothes when he is angry.

(int.) DOES that boy t*EAR* his clothes when he is angry?

Pasado

(af.) Mary t*ORE* a page from her book *yesterday*.
(María arrancó una página de su libro ayer.)

(neg.) Mary DID NOT t*ear* a page from her book *yesterday*.

(int.) DID Mary t*ear* a page from her book *yesterday?*

(af.) The dog *has* t*ORN* the curtains in the parlor.
(El perro ha desgarrado las cortinas en la sala.)

(neg.) The dog *has* NOT t*ORN* the curtains in the parlor.

(int.) *Has* the dog t*ORN* the curtains in the parlor?

Ejemplos ilustrativos de cómo emplear el verbo marcado con el número 3 en sus tiempos y formas fundamentales: clasificación *EAR, ORE, ORN.*

Infinitivo

That man likes *to* sw*EAR* in front of the children.
(A ese hombre le gusta blasfemar en frente de los niños.)

Presente

(af.) Those boys sw*EAR* in front of their teacher.
(Esos muchachos blasfeman en frente de su maestro.)

(neg.) Those boys DO NOT sw*EAR* in front of their teacher.

(int.) DO those boys sw*EAR* in front of their teacher?

Pasado

(af.) He sw*ORE* to tell the truth
(Él juró decir la verdad.)

(neg.) He DID NOT sw*ear* to tell the truth.

(int.) DID he sw*ear* to tell the truth?

Antepresente

(af.) You *have* sw*ORN* to tell the truth.
(Usted ha jurado decir la verdad.)

(neg.) You *have* NOT sw*ORN* to tell the truth.

(int.) *Have* you sw*ORN* to tell the truth?

Ejemplos ilustrativos de cómo emplear el verbo marcado con el número 4 en sus tiempos y formas fundamentales: clasificación *EAR, ORE, ORN*.

Infinitivo

We do not have *to* b*EAR* that noise.
(No tenemos que soportar ese ruido.)

Presente

(af.) You b*EAR* the pain without moaning.
(Tú soportas el dolor sin quejarte.)

(neg.) You DO NOT b*EAR* the pain without moaning.

(int.) DO you b*EAR* the pain without moaning?

Pasado

(af.) This apple-tree b*ORE* many apples *last year*.
(Este manzano dio muchas manzanas el año pasado.)

(neg.) This apple-tree DID NOT b*ear* many apples *last year*.

(int.) DID this apple-tree b*ear* many apples *last year?*

Antepresente

(af.) That female-dog *has* b*ORN* many little puppies.
(Esa perra ha parido muchos cachorritos.)

(neg.) That female-dog *has* NOT b*ORN* many little puppies.

(int.) *Has* that female-dog b*ORN* many little puppies?

Clasificación: *I-E, A-E, I-EN.*

Características: El rasgo común en el infinitivo es *i-e,* en el pasado *a-e* y en el participio pasado *i-en.*

Fonética Tanto la *i* del infinitivo como del participio pasado tienen casi el mismo sonido que en español, o sea, un sonido intermedio entre la *i* y la *e (i/e).*
En el infinitivo y el pasado la *e* es muda y en éste la vocal *a* se pronuncia *ei,* en tanto que *en* suena igual que en castellano.

Infinitivo	Pasado	Participio Pasado
(I-E)	(A-E)	(I-EN)
1. *to* g*I*v*E* (dar)	g*A*v*E* (dió)	g*I*v*EN* (dado)
2. *to* forg*I*v*E* (perdonar)	forg*A*v*E* (perdonó)	rorg*I*v*EN* (perdonado)
3. *to* forb*I*d (prohibir)	forb*A*d*E* (prohibió)	forb*I*dd*EN* (prohibido)
4. *to* b*I*d (ofrecer, despedir*)	b*A*d*E* (ofreció, despidió)	b*I*dd*EN* (ofrecido, despedido)

Nota: Observe que *to forbid* y *to bid* no terminan en *e* en el infinitivo.

* To bid *farewell* significa despedirse.

Ejemplos ilustrativos de cómo emplear el verbo marcado con el número 1 en sus tiempos y formas fundamentales: clasificación *I-E, A-E, I-EN.*

Infinitivo

I am going *to* g*I*v*E* him a reward for his efforts.
(Voy a darle a él una recompensa por sus esfuerzos.)

Presente

(af.)   The boss g*I*v*E*s us many presents *every Christmas.*
(El jefe nos da muchos regalos cada navidad.)

(neg.) The boss DOES NOT g*I*v*E* us many presents *every Christmas.*

(int.) DOES the boss g*I*v*E* us many presents *every Christmas?*

Pasado

(af.) The manager g*A*v*E* him his profits sharing *last year.*
(El gerente le dio a él su reparto de utilidades el año pasado.)

(neg.) The manager DID NOT give him his profits sharing *last year.*

(int.) DID the manager give him his profits sharing *last year?*

Antepresente

(af.) Their father *has* g*I*v*EN* them very much money.
(Su padre les ha dado mucho dinero.)

(neg.) Their father *has* NOT g*I*v*EN* them very much money.

(int.) *Has* their father g*I*v*EN* them very much money?

Ejemplos ilustrativos de cómo emplear el verbo marcado con el número 2 en sus tiempos y formas fundamentales: clasificación *I-E, A-E, I-EN.*

Infinitivo

I beg you *to* forg*I*v*E* me for my delay.
(Le ruego me perdone por mi tardanza.)

Presente

(af.) Mother and father forg*I*v*E* our wrongdoings.
(Mamá y papá perdonan nuestras faltas.)

(neg.) Mother and father DO NOT forg*I*v*E* our wrongdoings.

(int.) DO mother and father forg*I*v*E* our wrongdoings?

Pasado

(af.) The teacher forg*A*v*E* John *yesterday.*
(El maestro perdonó a Juan ayer.)

(neg.) The teacher DID NOT forg*ive* John *yesterday*.

(int.) DID the teacher forg*ive* John *yesterday?*

Antepresente

(af.) Our father *has* forg*IvEN* our debts.
(Nuestro padre ha perdonado nuestras deudas.)

(neg.) Our father *has* NOT forg*IvEN* our debts.

(int.) *Has* our father forg*IvEN* our debts?

Ejemplos ilustrativos de cómo emplear el verbo marcado cor.
el número 3 en sus tiempos y formas fundamentales: clasificación *I-E, A-E, I-EN*.

Infinitivo

The principal will have *to* forb*Id* smoking in school.
(El director tendrá que prohibir fumar en la escuela.)

Presente

(af.) The teacher forb*Ids* conversation in the classroom.
(El maestro prohíbe la conversación en el aula.)

(neg.) The teacher DOES NOT forb*Id* conversation in the classroom.

(int.) DOES the teacher forb*Id* conversation in the classroom?

Pasado

(af.) The doctor forb*AdE* him liquor and tobacco.
(El doctor le prohibió a él el licor y el tabaco.)

(neg.) The doctor DID NOT forb*id* him liquor and tobacco.

(int.) DID the doctor forb*id* him liquor and tobacco?

Antepresente

(af.) He *has* forb*IddEN* us to smoke in school.
(Él nos ha prohibido fumar en la escuela.)

(neg.) He *has* NOT forb*IddEN* us to smoke in school.

(int.) *Has* he forb*IddEN* us to smoke in school?

Ejemplos ilustrativos de cómo emplear el verbo marcado con el número 4 en sus tiempos y formas fundamentales: clasificación *I-E, A-E, I-EN*.

Infinitivo

He likes *to* b*I*d in the auctions.
(A él le gusta ofrecer en las subastas.)

Presente

(af.) Robert b*I*ds farewell to his friends when he goes away.
(Roberto se despide de sus amigos cuando él se aleja.)

(neg.) Robert DOES NOT b*I*d farewell to his friends when he goes away.

(int.) DOES Robert b*I*d farewell to his friends when he goes away?

Pasado

(af.) That man b*A*d*E* too much in the auction *yesterday.*
(Ese hombre ofreció demasiado en la subasta ayer.)

(neg.) That man DID NOT b*i*d too much in the auction *yesterday.*

(int.) DID that man b*i*d too much in the auction *yesterday?*

Antepresente

(af.) That bidder *has* b*I*dd*EN* high amounts of money.
(Ese postor ha ofrecido altas cantidades de dinero.)

(neg.) That bidder *has* NOT b*I*dd*EN* high amounts of money.

(int.) *Has* that bidder b*I*dd*EN* high amounts of money?

141

Clasificación: *ET, OT, OTTEN.*

Características: Infinitivo *et;* pasado *ot;* y participio pasado *otten.*

Fonética: Igual que en español excepto la *g* que se pronuncia como en *gato.* La primera *e* en *to beget* tiene sonido de *i* latina.

Infinitivo	Pasado	Participio Pasado
(ET)	*(OT)*	*(OTTEN)*
1. *to* g*ET* (conseguir)	g*OT* (consiguió)	g*OTTEN* (o g*ot*) (conseguido)
2. *to* forg*ET* (olvidar)	forg*OT* (olvidó)	forg*OTTEN* (olvidado)
3. *to* beg*ET* (engendrar, causar)	beg*OT* (engendró, causó)	beg*OTTEN* (engendrado, causado)

Sub-clasificación: *EN* (participio pasado).

Características: El rasgo afín en el participio pasado es la terminación *EN.*

Fonética: Pronúnciese *ea* como *i* latina y la *a* de *ate* con sonido *ei.* En *fall, fallen* la *a* suena como *o* y la *ll* como *l* castellana.

Infinitivo	Pasado	Participio Pasado
		(EN)
1. *to* e*at* (comer)	ate (comió)	eat*EN* (comido)
2. *to* fall (caer)	fell (cayó	fall*EN* (caído)

Ejemplos ilustrativos de cómo emplear el verbo marcado con el número 1 en sus tiempos y formas fundamentales: clasificación *ET, OT, OTTEN.*

Infinitivo

They would like *to* g*ET* a good price.
(A ellos les gustaría conseguir un buen precio.)

Presente

(af.)   I g*ET* good profits *every year.*
(Yo consigo buenas utilidades todos los años.)

(neg.)   I DO NOT g*ET* profits *every year.*

(int.)   DO I g*ET* good profits *every year?*

Pasado

(af.)   John g*OT* a ten per cent discount in that purchase.
(Juan consiguió un diez por ciento de descuento en esa compra.)

(neg.)   John DID NOT *get* a ten per cent discount in that purchase.

(int.)   DID John *get* a ten per cent discount in that purchase?

Antepresente

(af.)   They *have* g*OTTEN* (o *got*) two seats for the theater.
(Ellos han conseguido dos asientos para el teatro.)

(neg.)   They *have* NOT g*OTTEN* (o *got*) two seats for the theater.

(int.)   *Have* they g*OTTEN* (o *got*) two seats for the theater?

Ejemplos ilustrativos de cómo emplear el verbo marcado con el número 2 en sus tiempos y formas fundamentales: clasificación *ET, OT, OTTEN.*

Infinitivo

She is trying *to* forg*ET* that horrible accident.
(Ella está tratando de olvidar ese horrible accidente.)

Presente

(af.) I forg*ET* my keys when I am in a hurry.
(Yo olvido mis llaves cuando estoy de prisa.)

(neg.) I DO NOT forg*ET* my keys when I ham in a hurry.

(int.) DO I forg*ET* my keys when I am in a hurry?

Pasado

(af.) He forg*OT* to bring his camera *yesterday*.
(Él olvidó traer su cámara ayer.)

(neg.) He DID NOT forg*et* to bring his camera *yesterday*.

(int.) DID he forg*et* to bring his camera *yesterday?*

Antepresente

(af.) Mary *has* forg*OTTEN* her teacher's address.
(María ha olvidado la dirección de su maestra.)

(neg.) Mary *has* NOT forg*OTTEN* her teacher's address.

(int.) *Has* Mary forg*OTTEN* her teacher's address?

Ejemplos ilustrativos de cómo emplear el verbo marcado con el número 3 en sus tiempos y formas fundamentales: clasificación *ET, OT, OTTEN.*

Infinitivo

That stallion will have *to* beg*ET* fine horses.
(Ese caballo padre tendrá que engendrar magníficos caballos.)

Presente

(af.) This bull beg*ET*s fine specimens.
(Este toro engendra magníficos ejemplares.)

(neg.) This bull DOES NOT beg*ET* fine specimens.

(int.) DOES this bull beg*ET* fine specimens?

Pasado

(af.) That patriarch beg*OT* many children.
(Ese patriarca engendró muchos hijos.)

(neg.)   That patriarch DID NOT beg*et* many children.

(int.)   DID that patriarch beg*et* many children?

Antepresente

(af.,   This stallion *has* beg*OTTEN* a lot of specimens.
         (Este caballo padre ha engendrado muchos ejemplares.)

(neg.)   This stallion *has* NOT beg*OTTEN* a lot of specimens.

(int.)   *Has* this stallion beg*OTTEN* a lot of specimens?

Ejemplos ilustrativos de cómo emplear el verbo marcado con el número 1 en sus tiempos y formas fundamentales sub-clasificación *EN* (participio pasado).

Infinitivo

I would like *to* eat chicken salad.
(Me gustaría comer ensalada de pollo.)

Presente

(af.)   They eat dinner in a restaurant *every day*.
         (Ellos comen en un restaurante todos los días.)

(neg.)   They DO NOT eat dinner in a restaurant *every day*.

(int.)   DO they eat dinner in a restaurant *every day?*

Pasado

(af.)   John ate pork chops *yesterday*.
         (Juan comió chuletas de puerco ayer.)

(neg.)   John DID NOT eat pork chops *yesterday*.

(int.)   DID John eat pork chops *yesterday?*

Antepresente

(af.)   We *have* eat*EN* shrimps *many times*.
         (Hemos comido camarones muchas veces.)

(neg.)   We *have* NOT eat*EN* shrimps *many times*.

(int.)   *Have* we eat*EN* shrimps *many times?*

Ejemplos ilustrativos de cómo emplear el verbo marcado con el número 2 en sus tiempos y formas fundamentales: sub-clasificación *EN* (participio pasado).

Infinitivo

He is going *to* fall if he keeps on skating.
(Él va a caerse si sigue patinando.)

Presente

(af.)   Henry falls when he skates.
(Enrique se cae cuando patina.)

(neg.) Henry DOES NOT fall when he skates.

(int.) DOES Henry fall when he skates?

Pasado

(af.)   Henry fell when he was skating *yesterday*.
(Enrique se cayó cuando estaba patinando ayer.)

(neg.) Henry DID NOT fall when he was skating *yesterday*

(int.) DID Henry fall when he was skating *yesterday?*

Antepresente

(af.)   He *has* fall*EN many times* while skating.
(Él se ha caído muchas veces al patinar.)

(neg.) He *has* NOT fall*EN many times* while skating.

(int.) *Has* he fall*EN many times* while skating?

Clasificación: *OME, AME, OME.*

Características: El rasgo afín en el infinitivo son las letras *ome;* en el pasado *ame* y en el participio pasado *ome.*
Nótese que el rasgo del infinitivo y el participio pasado son idénticos.

Fonética: Pronúnciese *om, eim, om* respectivamente las letras afines.

Infinitivo	*Pasado*	*Participio Pasado*
(OME)	*(AME)*	*(OME)*
1. *to* cOME (venir)	cAME (vino)	cOME (venido)
2. *to* becOME* (llegar a ser, volverse)	becAME (llegó a ser, se volvió)	becOME (llegado a ser, convertido)
3. *to* overcOME (sobreponerse, triunfar sobre)	overcAME (se sobrepuso, triunfó sobre)	overcOME (sobrepuesto, triunfado sobre)

* El verbo *to become* cuando va seguido de algunos adjetivos adquiere distintos significados. Ejemplos:

> to become *impatient* = impacientarse
> to become *angry* = enojarse
> to become *rich* = enriquecerse
> to become *crazy* = volverse loco
> to become *red* = sonrojarse

Ejemplos ilustrativos de cómo emplear el verbo marcado con el número 1 en sus tiempos y formas fundamentales: clasificación *OME, AME, OME.*

Infinitivo

They like *to* cOME here on week-ends.
(A ellos les gusta venir aquí los fines de semana.)

147

Presente

(af.) My friends c*OME* for dinner on Sundays.
       (Mis amigos vienen a comer los domingos.)

(neg.) My friends DO NOT c*OME* for dinner on Sundays.

(int.) DO my friends c*OME* for dinner on Sundays?

Pasado

(af.) Henry c*AME* here *yesterday*.
       (Enrique vino aquí ayer.)

(neg.) Henry DID NOT *come* here *yesterday*.

(int.) DID Henry *come* here *yesterday*?

Antepresente

(af.) The tourists *have* c*OME* to this place *many times*.
       (Los turistas han venido a este lugar muchas veces.)

(neg.) The tourists *have* NOT c*OME* to this place *many times*.

(int.) *Have* the tourists c*OME* to this place *many times*?

Ejemplos ilustrativos de cómo emplear el verbo marcado con el número 2 en sus tiempos y formas fundamentales: clasificación *OME, AME, OME.*

Infinitivo

Paul wants *to* bec*OME* a lawyer.
(Pablo quiere llegar a ser abogado.)

Presente

(af.) They bec*OME* impatient with the children.
       (Ellos se impacientan con los niños.)

(neg.) They DO NOT bec*OME* impatient with the children.

(int.) DO they bec*OME* impatient with the children?

Pasado

(af.) Mr. Johnson bec*AME* president *last year*.
(El señor Johnson llegó a ser presidente el año pasado.)

(neg.) Mr. Johnson DID NOT bec*ome* president *last year*.

(int.) DID Mr. Johnson bec*ome* president *last year?*

Antepresente

(af.) My uncle *has* bec*OME* United States citizen.
(Mi tío ha llegado a ser ciudadano de los Estados Unidos.)

(neg.) My uncle *has* NOT bec*OME* United States citizen.

(int.) *Has* my uncle bec*OME* United States citizen?

Ejemplos ilustrativos de cómo emplear el verbo marcado con el número 3 en sus tiempos y formas fundamentales: clasificación *OME, AME, OME.*

Infinitivo

You have *to* overc*OME* pain.
(Tienes que sobreponerte al dolor.)

Presente

(af.) I overc*OME* fear during earthquakes.
(Me sobrepongo al miedo durante los temblores de tierra.)

(neg.) I DO NOT overc*OME* fear during earthquakes.

(int.) DO I overc*OME* fear during earthquakes?

Pasado

(af.) He overc*AME* pain after his operation.
(Él se sobrepuso al dolor después de su operación.)

(neg.) He DID NOT overc*ome* pain after his operation.

(int.) DID he overc*ome* pain after his operation?

Antepresente

(af.)   Robert *has* overc*OME* his handicap.
        (Roberto ha triunfado sobre su defecto físico.)

(neg.)   Robert *has* NOT overc*OME* his handicap.

(int.)   *Has* Robert overc*OME* his handicap?

Clasificaciones: *A, B* y *C* (Afinidad en el Participio Pasado solamente).

Características: Las tres clasificaciones *A, B* y *C* son desafines entre sí en el presente y pasado. La primera tiene como rasgo mnemotécnico la terminación *AIN* en sus participios pasados. La segunda, la terminación *EEN*. Y la tercera *ONE* en el participio pasado y *O* que es común en el infinitivo.

Fonética: Pronúnciese *ein, in* y *on* respectivamente dichos rasgos mnemotécnicos.

Infinitivo	Pasado	Participio Pasado AIN	
1. *to* lie (yacer, tenderse)	lay (yació, se tendió)	l*AIN* (yacido, tendido)	A
2. *to* slay (matar)	slew (mató)	sl*AIN* (matado)	

Infinitivo	Pasado	Participio Pasado EEN	
1. *to* be (ser, estar)	was (era, estaba, estuvo) were (eran, estaban, estuvieron)	b*EEN* (sido, estado)	B
2. *to* see (ver)	saw (vio)	s*EEN* (visto)	
3. *to* foresee (prever)	foresaw (previó)	fores*EEN* (previsto)	

Infinitivo	Pasado	Participio Pasado ONE	
1. *to* d*O* (hacer)	did (hizo)	d*ONE* (hecho)	C
2. *to* g*O* (ir)	went (fue)	g*ONE* (ido)	
3. *to* underg*O* (someterse a, experimentar)	underwent (se sometió, experimentó)	underg*ONE* (sometido, experimentado)	

Ejemplos ilustrativos de cómo emplear el verbo marcado con el número 1 en sus tiempos y formas fundamentales: clasificación *A*.

Infinitivo

He had *to* lie on the floor during the shooting.
(Él tuvo que tenderse en el piso durante el tiroteo.)

Presente

(af.) Mr. Taylor's tomb lies in the National Cementery.
(La tumba del señor Taylor está en el Cementerio Nacional.)

(neg.) Mr. Taylor's tomb DOES NOT lie in the National Cementery.

(int.) DOES Mr. Taylor's tomb lie in the National Cementery?

Pasado

(af.) He lay unconscious when he was hurt.
(Él yació inconsciente cuando fue herido.)

(neg.) He DID NOT *lie* unconscious when he was hurt.

(int.) DID he *lie* unconscious when he was hurt?

Antepresente

(af.) The dead body *has* lAIN on the floor for hours.
(El cadáver ha yacido en el piso por horas.)

(neg.) The dead body *has* NOT lAIN on the floor for hours.

(int.) *Has* the dead body lAIN on the floor for hours?

Ejemplos ilustrativos de cómo emplear el verbo marcado con el número 2 en sus tiempos y formas fundamentales: clasificación *A*.

Infinitivo

He didn't have *to* slay that man.
(Él no tenía que matar a ese hombre.)
152

Presente

(af.)   They slay innocent people.
        (Ellos matan a gente inocente.)

(neg.) They DO NOT slay innocent people.

(int.)   DO they slay innocent people?

Pasado

(af.)   He slew a man *last week.*
        (Él le quitó la vida a un hombre la semana pasada.)

(neg.) He DID NOT *slay* a man *last week.*

(int.)   DID he *slay* a man *last week?*

Antepresente

(af.)   They *have* slAIN many innocent people during the war.
        (Ellos han matado a muchas personas inocentes durante la guerra.)

(neg.) They *have* NOT slAIN many innocent people during the war.

(int.)   *Have* they slAIN many innocent people during the war?

Ejemplos ilustrativos de cómo emplear el verbo marcado con el número 1 en sus tiempos y formas fundamentales: clasif:cación *B*.

Infinitivo

We have *to* be prepared in case of emergency.
(Tenemos que estar preparados en caso de emergencia.)

Presente

(af.)   Henry *IS* busy *in the morning.*
        (Enrique está ocupado en la mañana.)

(neg.) Henry *IS* NOT busy *in the morning.*

(int.)   *IS* Henry busy *in the morning?*

Pasado

(af.) Alice *WAS* sick *yesterday*.
(Alicia estuvo enferma ayer.)

(neg.) Alice *WAS* NOT sick *yesterday*.

(int.) *WAS* Alice sick *yesterday?*

Antepresente

(af.) They *have* b*EEN* friends *since a long time ago*.
(Ellos han sido amigos desde hace muchos años.)

(neg.) They *have* NOT b*EEN* friends *since a long time ago*.

(int.) *Have* they b*EEN* friends *since a long time ago?*

Ejemplos ilustrativos de cómo emplear el verbo marcado con el número 2 en sus tiempos y formas fundamentales: clasificación *B*.

Infinitivo

She would like *to* she her Mexican friends again.
(A ella le gustaría ver a sus amigos mexicanos otra vez.)

Presente

(af.) They see him very *often*.
(Ellos lo ven muy seguido.)

(neg.) They DO NOT see him very *often*.

(int.) DO they see him very *often?*

Pasado

(af.) Mary saw Charles *yesterday*.
(María vio a Carlos ayer.)

(neg.) Mary DID NOT *see* Charles *yesterday*.

(int.) DID Mary *see* Charles *yesterday?*

Antepresente

(af.) We *have* s*EEN* many cow-boy pictures.
(Hemos visto muchas películas de vaqueros.)

(neg.) We *have* NOT s*EEN* many cow-boy pictures.

(int.) *Have* we s*EEN* many cow-boy pictures?

Ejemplos ilustrativos de cómo emplear el verbo marcado con el número 3 en sus tiempos y formas fundamentales: clasificación *B*.

Infinitivo

You have *to* foresee unexpected accidents.
(Usted tiene que prever accidentes inesperados.)

Presente

(af.) The chief engineer foresees everything at the plant.
(El ingeniero en jefe preve todo en la planta.)

(neg.) The chief engineer DOES NOT foresee everything at the plant.

(int.) DOES the chief engineer foresee everything at the plant?

Pasado

(af.) He foresaw every detail in the maintenance department.
(Él previó todos los detalles en el departamento de mantenimiento.)

(neg.) He DID NOT *foresee* every detail in the maintenance department.

(int.) DID the *foresee* every detail in the maintenance department?

Antepresente

(af.) He *has* fores*EEN* every work accident.
(Él ha previsto todos los accidentes de trabajo.)

(neg.) He *has* NOT fores*EEN* every work accident.

(int.) *Has* he fores*EEN* every work accident?

Ejemplos ilustrativos de cómo emplear el verbo marcado con el número 1 en sus tiempos y formas fundamentales: clasificación *C*.

Infinitivo

I have *to* do this assignment right now.
(Tengo que hacer esta asignación en seguida.)

Presente

(af.) Some housewives do their chores *every day.*
(Algunas amas de casa hacen sus labores domésticos todos los días.)

(neg.) Some housewives DO NOT do their chores *every day.*

(int.) DO some housewives do their chores *every day?*

Pasado

(af.) Helen did her home-work *last night.*
(Elena hizo su tarea anoche.)

(neg.) Helen DID NOT do her home-work *last night.*

(int.) DID Helen do her home-work *last night?*

Antepresente

(af.) They *have* dONE a good work *lately.*
(Ellos han hecho un buen trabajo últimamente.)

(neg.) They *have* NOT dONE a good work *lately.*

(int.) *Have* they dONE a good work *lately?*

Ejemplos ilustrativos de cómo emplear el verbo marcado con el número 2 en sus tiempos y formas fundamentales: clasificación *C.*

Infinitivo

I wish *to go* to a picnic next Sunday.
(Deseo ir a un día de campo el próximo domingo.)

Presente

(af.) Some students go to school on Saturday.
(Algunos estudiantes van a la escuela el sábado.)

(neg.) Some students DO NOT go to school on Saturday.

(int.) DO some students go to school on Saturday?

Pasado

(af.) John went to New York *last year.*
(Juan fue a Nueva York el año pasado.)

156

(neg.)	John DID NOT *go* to New York *last year.*
(int.)	DID John *go* to New York *last year?*

Antepresente

(af.)	They *have* gONE to the theater.
	(Ellos han ido al teatro.)
(neg.)	They *have* NOT gONE to the theater.
(int.)	*Have* they gONE to the theater?

Ejemplos ilustrativos de cómo emplear el verbo marcado con el número 3 en sus tiempos y formas fundamentales: clasificación *C.*

Infinitivo

He does not want *to* undergo that surgical operation.
(Él no quiere someterse a esa operación quirúrgica.)

Presente

(af.)	My aunt undergoes medical treatments very *often.*
	(Mi tía se somete a tratamientos médicos muy seguido.)
(neg.)	My aunt DOES NOT undergo medical treatments very *often.*
(int.)	DOES my aunt undergo medical treatments very *often?*

Pasado

(af.)	Paul underwent a surgical operation *last week.*
	(Pablo se sometió a una operación quirúrgica la semana pasada.)
(neg.)	Paul DID NOT undergo a surgical operation *last week.*
(int.)	DID Paul undergo a surgical operation *last week?*

Antepresente

(af.)	She *has* undergONE two surgical operations.
	(Ella se ha sometido a dos operaciones quirúrgicas.)
(neg.)	She *has* NOT undergONE two surgical operations.
(int.)	*Has* she undergONE two surgical operations?

TERCER GRUPO

VERBOS CON FORMAS IDÉNTICAS EN EL INFINITIVO, PASADO Y PARTICIPIO PASADO

Clasificación: *ET, ET, ET* con variantes *EAD* y *EAT*.

Características: La combinación *et* es el rasgo común en sus tres formas excepto en *to spread, to sweat* y *to beat*.

Fonética: Pronúnciese *et* esta característica común. Las vocales *ea* en *spread* y *sweat* tienen sonido de *e* castellana, en tanto que la combinación *ea* en *beat* suena *i*. Sin embargo, advierta que en todos estos verbos predomina el sonido de la vocal *e*, excluyendo a *to beat*.

Infinitivo	Pasado	Participio Pasado
1. *to* l*ET* (dejar, permitir)	l*ET* (dejó, permitió)	l*ET* (dejado, permitido)
2. *to* s*ET* (fijar, poner)	s*ET* (fijó, puso)	s*ET* (fijado, puesto)
3. *to* w*ET* (mojar, humedecer)	w*ET* (mojó, humedeció)	w*ET* (mojado, humedecido)
4. *to* b*ET* (apostar)	b*ET* (apostó)	b*ET* (apostado)
5. *to* spr*EAD* (extender, desplegar)	spr*EAD* (extendió, desplegó)	spr*EAD* (extendido, desplegado)
6. *to* sw*EAT** (sudar)	sw*EAT* (sudó)	sw*EAT* (sudado)
7. *to* b*EAT*** (batir, golpear, vencer)	b*EAT* (batió, golpeó, venció)	b*EAT* (batido, golpeado, vencido)

* Este verbo puede también ser regular (to sweat-sweat*ed*).

** Su participio pasado también puede ser b*eaten*. Por otra parte, *to beat* puede significar asimismo *latir* (the heart *beats*: late el corazón) al igual que *tocar* (*to beat* the drum: tocar el tambor).

Ejemplos ilustrativos de cómo emplear el verbo marcado con el número 1 en sus tiempos y formas fundamentales: clasificación *ET, ET, ET*.

Infinitivo

I am going *to* l*ET* you use my English book.
(Te voy a permitir usar mi libro de inglés.)

Presente

(af.) I l*ET* my friends play in the backyard.
(Yo dejo a mis amigos jugar en el patio trasero.)

(neg.) I DO NOT l*ET* my friends play in the backyard.

(int.) DO I l*ET* my friends play in the backyard?

Pasado

(af.) The teacher l*ET* him go home early *yesterday*.
(El maestro le permitió a él ir a su casa temprano ayer.)

(neg.) The teacher DID NOT *let* him go home early *yesterday*.

(int.) DID the teacher *let* him go home early *yesterday*?

Antepresente

(af.) Our parents *have* l*ET* us travel during the Summer.
(Nuestros padres nos han dejado viajar durante el verano.)

(neg.) Our parents *have* NOT l*ET* us travel during the Summer.

(int.) *Have* our parents l*ET* us travel during the Summer?

Ejemplos ilustrativos de cómo emplear el verbo marcado con el número 2 en sus tiempos y formas fundamentales: clasificación *ET, ET, ET*.

Infinitivo

The manager is going *to* s*ET* the date for the next meeting.
(El gerente va a fijar la fecha para la próxima junta.)

Presente

(af.)   Mary s*ET*s the table *every day*.
         (María pone la mesa todos los días.)

(neg.)   Mary DOES NOT s*ET* the table *every day*.

(int.)   DOES Mary s*ET* the table *every day?*

Pasado

(af.)   You s*ET* the clock on time *yesterday*.
         (Usted puso el reloj en hora ayer.)

(neg.)   You DID NOT s*et* the clock on time *yesterday*.

(int.)   DID you s*et* the clock on time *yesterday?*

Antepresente

(af.)   They *have* s*ET* the date for the next meeting.
         (Ellos han fijado la fecha para la próxima junta.)

(neg.)   They *have* NOT s*ET* the date for the next meeting.

(int.)   *Have* they s*ET* the date for the next meeting?

Ejemplos ilustrativos de cómo emplear el verbo marcado con el número 3 en sus tiempos y formas fundamentales: clasificación *ET, ET, ET*.

Infinitivo

I think this rain is going *to* w*ET* the dry fields soon.
(Yo creo que esta lluvia va a mojar los campos secos pronto.)

Presente

(af.)   The rains w*ET* this region during this season.
         (Las lluvias mojan esta región durante esta estación.)

(neg.)   The rains DO NOT w*ET* this region during this season.

(int.)   DO the rains w*ET* this region during this season?

Pasado

(af.)   The gardener *w*ET** the grass *last week*.
         (El jardinero mojó el césped la semana pasada.)

(neg.)   The gardener DID NOT w*et* the grass *last week.*

(int.)   DID the gardener w*et* the grass *last week?*

Antepresente

(af.)   The woman *has* w*ET* the clothes before ironing them.
(La mujer ha humedecido la ropa antes de plancharla.)

(neg.)   The woman *has* NOT w*ET* the clothes before ironing them?

(int.)   *Has* the woman w*ET* the clothes before ironing them?

Ejemplos ilustrativos de cómo emplear el verbo marcado con el número 4 en sus tiempos y formas fundamentales: clasificación *ET, ET, ET.*

Infinitivo

He likes *to* b*ET* money in the horse races.
(A él le gusta apostar dinero en las carreras de caballos.)

Presente

(af.)   Some gamblers b*ET* money in *every* horse-race.
(Algunos jugadores apuestan dinero en todas las carreras de caballos.)

(neg.)   Some gamblers DO NOT b*ET* money in *every* horse-race.

(int.)   DO some gamblers b*ET* money in *every* horse-race?

Pasado

(af.)   He b*ET* too much money in the *last* race.
(Él apostó demasiado dinero en la última carrera.)

(neg.)   He DID NOT b*et* too much money in the *last* race.

(int.)   DID he b*et* too much money in the *last* race?

Antepresente

(af.)   John *has* b*ET* them very much money in the horse-races.
(Juan les ha apostado mucho dinero en las carreras de caballos.)

161

(neg.) John *has* NOT b*ET* them very much money in the horse-races.

(int.) *Has* John b*ET* them very much money in the horse-races?

Ejemplos ilustrativos de cómo emplear el verbo marcado con el número 5 en sus tiempos y formas fundamentales: clasificación *ET*, *ET*, *ET*.

Variante: *EAD*, *EAD*, *EAD*.

Infinitivo

The dying eagle was trying *to* spr*EAD* its wings in vain. (El águila moribunda estaba tratando de extender sus alas en vano.)

Presente

(af.) Some birds spr*EAD* their wings as they fly. (Algunas aves extienden las alas cuando vuelan.)

(neg.) Some birds DO NOT spr*EAD* their wings as they fly.

(int.) DO some birds spr*EAD* their wings as they fly?

Pasado

(af.) The epidemic spr*EAD* over the city very quickly. (La epidemia se extendió sobre la ciudad muy rápidamente.)

(neg.) The epidemic DID NOT spr*ead* over the city very quickly.

(int.) DID the epidemic spr*ead* over the city very quickly?

Antepresente

(af.) The infection *has* spr*EAD* all over his wound. (La infección se ha extendido por toda su herida.)

162

(neg.) The infection *has* NOT spr*EAD* all over his wound.

(int.) *Has* the infection spr*EAD* all over his wound?

Ejemplos ilustrativos de cómo emplear el verbo marcado con el número 6 en sus tiempos y formas fundamentales: clasificación: *ET, ET, ET*.

Variante: *EAT, EAT, EAT*.

Infinitivo

You are going *to* sw*EAT* very much in that hot weather. (Tú vas a sudar mucho en ese clima caliente.)

Presente

(af.) I sw*EAT* very much *during the Summer*. (Yo sudo mucho durante el verano.)

(neg.) I DO NOT sw*EAT* very much *during the Summer*.

(int.) DO I sw*EAT* very much *during the Summer?*

Pasado

(af.) You sw*EAT* a lot in that crowded bus *yesterday*. (Usted sudó mucho en ese autobús atestado ayer.)

(neg.) You DID NOT sw*eat* a lot in that crowded bus *yesterday*.

(int.) DID you sw*eat* a lot in that crowded bus *yesterday?*

Antepresente

(af.) We *have* sw*EAT* a great deal *during this mountain-climbing*. (Hemos sudado mucho durante la ascensión de esta montaña.)

(neg.) We *have* NOT sw*EAT* a great deal *during this mountain-climbing*.

(int.) *Have* we sw*EAT* a great deal *during this mountain-climbing?*

Ejemplos ilustrativos de cómo emplear el verbo marcado con el número 7 en sus tiempos y formas fundamentales: clasificación *ET, ET, ET*.

Variante: *EAT, EAT, EAT*.

Infinitivo

Mary likes *to* b*EAT* the eggs for the cake.
(A María le gusta batir los huevos para el pastel.)

Presente

(af.)   Henry b*EAT*s the drum in the school band.
(Enrique toca el tambor en la banda de la escuela.)

(neg.)   Henry DOES NOT b*EAT* the drum in the school band.

(int.)   DOES Henry b*EAT* the drum in the school band?

Pasado

(af.)   The world's champion b*EAT* his foe in the first round.
(El campeón mundial venció a su oponente en el primer asalto.)

(neg.)   The world's champion DID NOT b*eat* his foe in the first round.

(int.)   DID the world's champion b*eat* his foe in the first round?

Antepresente

(af.)   That man *has* b*EAT* (b*eaten*) his wife *many times*.
(Ese hombre ha golpeado a su esposa muchas veces.)

(neg.)   That man *has* NOT b*EAT* (b*eaten*) his wife *many times*.

(int.)   *Has* that man b*EAT* (b*eaten*) his wife *many times?*

Clasificación: *IT, IT, IT.*

Características: La combinación *IT* es el rasgo común en sus tres formas.

Fonética: Pronúnciese la vocal *i* con sonido intermedio entre la *i* y la *e*, o sea, con la abertura bucal de la *i* pero emitiendo el sonido de la *e*. En suma, dicha combinación *IT* se pronuncia igual que el pronombre *it*.

Infinitivo	Pasado	Participio Pasado
1. *to* h*IT* (pegar, golpear)	h*IT* (pegó, golpeó)	h*IT* (pegado, golpeado)
2. *to* qu*IT* (dejar de, renunciar)	qu*IT* (dejó de, renunció)	qu*IT* (dejado de, renunciado)
3. *to* sp*IT* (escupir)	sp*IT* (escupió)	sp*IT* (escupido)
4. *to* spl*IT* (dividir)	spl*IT* (dividió)	spl*IT* (dividido)

Sub-clasificación: *ID, ID, ID.*

Infinitivo	Pasado	Participio Pasado
1. *to* b*ID* (ofrecer, despedirse)*	b*ID* (ofreció, despidió)*	b*ID* (ofrecido, despedido)*
2. *to* get r*ID* (deshacerse, librarse)**	got r*ID* (se deshizo, se libró)	got r*ID* (deshecho, librado)

* *To bid farewell* significa *despedirse,* o sea, sólo cuando se combinan estas dos palabras. Recuérdese que *to bid* se halla también agrupado en la clasificación *I-E, A-E, I-EN: to bid, bade, bidden.*

** *To get rid* es un verbo reflexivo cuya radical es *to get, got, got* o *gotten.* Es por lo tanto un verbo compuesto que se apega al patrón de su radical. Por otra parte, existe también el verbo *to rid, rid, rid* pero no es reflexivo y el cual significa *librar, quitar de encima.*

Ejemplos ilustrativos de cómo emplear el verbo marcado con el número 1 en sus tiempos y formas fundamentales: clasificación *IT, IT IT.*

Infinitivo

Robert likes *to* h*I*T the ball with his bat.
(A Roberto le gusta pegarle a la pelota con su bate.)

Presente

(af.)   The boys h*I*T the ball very hard when they play base-ball.
(Los muchachos golpean la pelota muy fuerte cuando juegan al beisbol.)

(neg.)   The boys DO NOT h*I*T the ball very hard when they play base-ball.

(int.)   DO the boys h*I*T the ball very hard when they play base-ball?

Pasado

(af.)   John h*I*T Peter with a stick *yesterday.*
(Juan le pegó a Pedro con un palo ayer.)

(neg.)   John DID NOT h*it* Peter a stick *yesterday.*

(int.)   DID John h*it* Peter with a stick *yesterday?*

Antepresente

(af.)   George *has* h*I*T little brother *many times.*
(Jorge le ha pegado a su hermanito muchas veces.)

(neg.)   George *has* NOT h*I*T little brother *many times.*

(int.)   *Has* George h*I*T his little brother *many :imes?*

Ejemplos ilustrativos de cómo emplear el verbo marcado con el número 2 en sus tiempos y formas fundamentales: clasificación *IT, IT, IT.*

Infinitivo

My brother is not going *to* qu*I*T his job.
(Mi hermano no va a renunciar a su empleo.)

Presente

(af.) You qu*I*T your jobs *often*.
(Tú renuncias a tus empleos muy seguido.)

(neg.) You DO NOT qu*I*T your jobs *very often*.

(int.) DO you qu*I*T your jobs *very often?*

Pasado

(af.) John qu*I*T smoking *last month*.
(Juan dejó de fumar el mes pasado.)

(neg.) John DID NOT qui*t* smoking *last month*.

(int.) DID John qui*t* smoking *last month?*

Antepresente

(af.) Mr. Taylor *has* qu*I*T his position.
(El señor Taylor ha renunciado a su puesto.)

(neg.) Mr. Taylor *has* NOT qu*I*T his position.

(int.) *Has* Mr. Taylor qu*I*T his position?

Ejemplos ilustrativos de cómo emplear el verbo marcado con el número 3 en sus tiempos y formas fundamentales: clasificación *IT, IT, IT*.

Infinitivo

You do not have *to* sp*I*T on the floor.
(Tú no tienes que escupir en el piso.)

Presente

(af.) Those students sp*I*T on the floor.
(Esos estudiantes escupen en el piso.)

(neg.) Those students DO NOT sp*I*T on the floor.

(int.) DO those students sp*I*T on the floor?

(af.)   He sp*IT* on the floor *yesterday*.
(Él escupió en el piso ayer.)

(neg.) He DID NOT sp*it* on the floor *yesterday*.

(int.) DID he sp*it* on the floor *yesterday?*

Antepresente

(af.)   He *has* sp*IT* on the floor *many times*.
(Él ha escupido en el piso muchas veces.)

(neg.) He *has* NOT sp*IT* on the floor *many times*.

(int.) *Has* he sp*IT* on the floor *many times?*

Ejemplos ilustrativos de cómo emplear el verbo marcado con el número 4 en sus tiempos y formas fundamentales: clasificación *IT, IT, IT.*

Infinitivo

He his going *to* spl*IT* the earnings tomorrow.
(Él va a dividir las ganancias mañana.)

Presente

(af.)   They spl*IT* the profits among themselves *every year*
(Ellos se dividen las utilidades cada año.)

(neg.) They DO NOT spl*IT* the profits among themselves *every year*.

(int.) DO they spl*IT* the profits among themselves *every year?*

Pasado

(af.)   Robert spl*IT* the money among his friends *yesterday*.
(Roberto dividió el dinero entre sus amigos ayer.)

(neg.) Robert DID NOT spl*it* the money among his friends *yesterday*.

(int.) DID Robert spl*it* the money among his friends *yesterday?*

Antepresente

(af.) They *have* splIT the profits among themselves.
(Ellos se han dividido las utilidades.)

(neg.) They *have* NOT splIT the profits among themselves.

(int.) *Have* they splIT the profits among themselves?

Ejemplos ilustrativos de cómo emplear el verbo marcado con el número 1 en sus tiempos y formas fundamentales: sub-clasificación *ID, ID, ID*.

Infinitivo

He likes *to* bID too much money in the auctions.
(A él le gusta ofrecer demasiado dinero en las subastas.)

Presente

(af.) You bID money in *every* auction.
(Usted ofrece dinero en cada subasta.)

(neg.) You DO NOT bID money in *every* auction.

(int.) DO you bID money in *every* auction?

Pasado

(af.) He bID a higher price *during the last* auction.
(Él ofreció un precio más alto durante la última subasta.)

(neg.) He DID NOT bid a higher price *during the last* auction.

(int.) DID he bid a higher price *during the last* auction?

Antepresente

(af.) Henry *has* bID farewell to all his friends.
(Enrique se ha despedido de todos sus amigos.)

(neg.) Henry *has* NOT bID farewell to all his friends.

(int.) *Has* Henry bID farewell to all his friends?

Ejemplos ilustrativos de cómo emplear el verbo marcado con el número 2 en sus tiempos y formas fundamentales: sub-clasificación *ID, ID, ID.*

Infinitivo

He is trying to get r*ID* of me.
(Él está tratando de deshacerse de mí.)

Presente

(af.) My aunt gets r*ID* of the mice *every month.*
(Mi tía se libra de los ratones cada mes.)

(neg.) My aunt DOES NOT get r*ID* of the mice *every month.*

(int.) DOES my aunt get r*ID* of the mice *every month?*

Pasado

(af.) They got r*ID* of all their old furniture.
(Ellos se deshicieron de todos sus muebles viejos.)

(neg.) They DID NOT get r*id* of all their old furniture.

(int.) DID they get r*id* of all their old furniture?

Antepresente

(af.) We *have* got r*ID* of the bugs at home.
(Nos hemos librado de los insectos en casa.)

(neg.) We *have* NOT got r*ID* of the bugs at home.

(int.) *Have* we got r*ID* of the bugs at home?

Clasificación: *U-T* u *O-T.*

Características: Las letras *u-t* y *o-t* son rasgos comunes en esta agrupación.

Fonética: Las vocales *u* y *o* tienen sonido de *o* española en la mayoría de los verbos. Solamente en *to put* suena como *u* y en *to hurt* y *to burst* como *e.*

Infinitivo	Pasado	Participio Pasado
1. *to* c*UT* (cortar, partir)	c*UT* (cortó, partió)	c*UT* (cortado, partido)
2. *to* sh*UT* (cerrar)	sh*UT* (cerró)	sh*UT* (cerrado)
3. *to* thr*UsT** (introducir, meter)	thr*UsT* (introdujo, metió)	thr*UsT* (introducido, metido)
4. *to* c*OsT* (costar)	c*OsT* (costó)	c*OsT* (costado)
5. *to* h*UrT* (herir, lastimar)	h*UrT* (hirió, lastimó)	h*UrT* (herido, lastimado)
6. *to* b*UrsT* (reventar, estallar)	b*UrsT* (reventó, estalló)	b*UrsT* (reventado, estallado)
7. *to* p*UT* (poner, colocar)	p*UT* (puso, colocó)	p*UT* (puesto, colocado)

* El sonido de *th* en *to thrust* es equivalente al de la *z* como se pronuncia en España: azul.

Ejemplos ilustrativos de cómo emplear el verbo marcado con el número 1 en sus tiempos y formas fundamentales: clasificación *U-T* u *O-T.*

Infinitivo

Alex likes *to* c*UT* wood for firewood.
(A Alejandro le gusta cortar madera para leña.)

Presente

(af.)   They c*UT* wood for firewood *every week.*
(Ellos cortan madera para leña cada semana.)

(neg.) They DO NOT c*UT* wood for firewood *every week.*

(int.) DO they c*UT* wood for firewood *every week?*

Pasado

(af.)   John c*UT* his finger *yesterday.*
(Juan se cortó el dedo ayer.)

(neg.) John DID NOT c*ut* his finger *yesterday.*

(int.) DID John c*ut* his finger *yesterday?*

Antepresente

(af.)   Alice *has* c*UT* the linen according to the pattern.
(Alicia ha cortado la tela de acuerdo con el patrón.)

(neg.) Alice *has* NOT c*UT* the linen according to the pattern.

(int.) *Has* Alice c*UT* the linen according to the pattern?

Ejemplos ilustrativos de cómo emplear el verbo marcado con el número 2 en sus tiempos y formas fundamentales: clasificación *U-T* u *O-T.*

Infinitivo

He will have *to* sh*UT* *up* right now.
(Él tendrá que callarse la boca ahora mismo.)

Presente

(af.)   I sh*UT* the door *every night.*
(Yo cierro la puerta todas las noches.)

(neg.) I DO NOT sh*UT* the door *every night.*

(int.) DO I sh*UT* the door *every night?*

172

Pasado

(af.)   Mary sh*UT* the window *last night*.
(María cerró la ventana anoche.)

(neg.) Mary DID NOT shut the window *last night*.

(int.) DID Mary shut the window *last night?*

Antepresente

(af.)   She *has* sh*UT* all the doors and windows.
(Ella ha cerrado todas las puertas y ventanas.)

(neg.) She *has* NOT sh*UT* all the doors and windows.

(int.) *Has* she sh*UT* all the door and windows?

Ejemplos ilustrativos de cómo emplear el verbo marcado con el número 3 en sus tiempos y formas fundamentales: clasificación *U-T* u *O-T*.

Infinitivo

He tried *to* thr*UsT* a knife into his enemy's back.
(Él intentó introducir un cuchillo en la espalda de su enemigo.)

Presente

(af.)   They thr*UsT* a sword to the bull in bull-fightings.
(Ellos le introducen una espada al toro en las corridas de toros.)

(neg.) They DO NOT thr*UsT* a sword to the bull in bull-fightings.

(int.) DO they thr*UsT* a sword to the bull in bull-fightings?

Pasado

(af.)   Paul thr*UsT* a coin in his pocket *yesterday*.
(Pablo se metió una moneda en su bolsillo ayer.)

(neg.) Paul DID NOT thrust a coin in his pocket *yesterday*.

(int.) DID Paul thrust a coin in his pocket *yesterday?*

173

(af.)   The doctors *have* thr*Us*T a tube in the patient's nose.
(Los médicos han introducido un tubo en la nariz del paciente.)

(neg.)   The doctors *have* NOT thr*Us*T a tube in the patient's nose.

(int.)   *Have* the doctors thr*Us*T a tube in the patient's nose?

Ejemplos ilustrativos de cómo emplear el verbo marcado con el número 4 en sus tiempos y formas fundamentales: clasificación *U-T* u *O-T*.

Infinitivo

That house is going *to* c*Os*T more than I figured.
(Esa casa va a costar más de lo que creí.)

Presente

(af.)   Grapes c*Os*T very cheap in this time of the year.
(Las uvas cuestan muy baratas en esta época del año.)

(neg.)   Grapes DO NOT c*Os*T very cheap in this time of the year.

(int.)   DO grapes c*Os*T very cheap in this time of the year?

Pasado

(af.)   This car c*Os*T five thousand dollars *last year*.
(Este auto costó cinco mil dólares el año pasado.)

(neg.)   This car DID NOT cost five thousand dollars *last year*.

(int.)   DID the this car cost five thousand dollars *last year*?

Antepresente

(af.)   These books *have* c*Os*T a lot of money.
(Estos libros han costado mucho dinero.)

(neg.)   These books *have* NOT c*Os*T a lot of money

(int.)   *Have* these books c*Os*T a lot of money?

Ejemplos ilustrativos de cómo emplear el verbo marcado con el número 5 en sus tiempos y formas fundamentales: clasificación *U-T* u *O-T*.

Infinitivo

You are going *to* hUrT yourself with that knife.
(Te vas a herir con esa navaja.)

Presente

(af.) Peter hUrTs his friends when they play together.
(Pedro lastima a sus amigos cuando juegan juntos.)

(neg.) Peter DOES NOT hUrT his friends when they play together.

(int.) DOES Peter hUrT his friends when they play together?

Pasado

(af.) Edward hUrT his arm *yesterday*.
(Eduardo se lastimó el brazo ayer.)

(neg.) Edward DID NOT hurt his arm *yesterday*.

(int.) DID Edward hUrT his arm *yesterday?*

Antepresente

(af.) Car drivers *have* hUrT many pedestrians *this year*.
(Los automovilistas han lesionado a muchos peatones este año.)

(neg.) Car drivers *have* NOT hUrT many pedestrians *this year*.

(int.) *Have* car divers hUrT many pedestrians *this year?*

Ejemplos ilustrativos de cómo emplear el verbo marcado con el número 6 en sus tiempos y formas fundamentales: clasificación *U-T* u *O-T*.

Infinitivo

That tire is probably going *to* bUrsT soon.
(Ese neumático probablemente va a reventar pronto.)

175

Presente

(af.) Those mines b*U*rs*T* very easily.
(Esas minas estallan muy fácilmente.)

(neg.) Those mines DO NOT b*U*rs*T* very easily.

(int.) DO those mines b*U*rs*T* very easily?

Pasado

(af.) Helen b*U*rs*T* *into* tears *yesterday*.
(Elena estalló en llanto ayer.) Lit: estalló en lágrimas.

(neg.) Helen DID NOT b*u*rs*t* *into* tears *yesterday*.

(int.) DID Helen b*u*rs*t* *into* tears *yesterday?*

Antepresente

(af.) Richard *has* b*U*rs*T* the door *open*.
(Ricardo ha abierto la puerta con violencia.)

(neg.) Richard *has* NOT b*U*rs*T* the door *open*.

(int.) *Has* Richard b*U*rs*T* the door *open?*

Ejemplos ilustrativos de cómo emplear el verbo marcado con el número 7 en sus tiempos y formas fundamentales: clasificación *U-T* u *O-T*.

Infinitivo

You do not have *to* p*U*T your books on that table.
(Tú no tienes que poner tus libros en esa mesa.)

Presente

(af.) I p*U*T my clothes on that chair.
(Yo pongo mi ropa en esa silla.)

(neg.) I DO NOT p*U*T my clothes on that chair.

(int.) DO I p*U*T my clothes on that chair?

176

(af.)   The manager p*UT* the contract on his desk.
        (El gerente puso el contrato sobre el escritorio.)

(neg.) The manager DID NOT p*ut* the contract on his desk.

(int.) DID the manager p*ut* the contract on his desk?

Antepresente

(af.)   They *have* p*UT on* their shoes in a hurry.
        (Ellos se han puesto los zapatos de prisa.)

(neg.) They *have* NOT p*UT on* their shoes in a hurry.

(int.) *Have* they p*UT* on their shoes in a hurry?

Clasificación: *CAST, CAST, CAST.*

Características: Las letras *cast* son el rasgo común en este grupo.

Fonética: El sonido de estas letras es igual que el que tienen en castellano.

Infinitivo	Pasado	Participio Pasado
1. *to* CAST (tirar, arrojar, echar)	CAST (tiró, arrojó, echó)	CAST (tirado, arrojado, echado)
2. *to* broad*CAST***** (difundir)	broad*CAST* (difundió)	broad*CAST* (difundido)
3. *to* fore*CAST***** (predecir)	fore*CAST* (difundió)	fore*CAST* (predicho)

* Los verbos *to broadcast* y *to forecast* también pueden ser regulares: *broadcastED, forecastED.*

Ejemplos ilustrativos de cómo emplear el verbo marcado con el número 1 en sus tiempos y formas fundamentales: clasificación *CAST, CAST, CAST.*

Infinitivo

You do not have *to* CAST stones to anybody.
(Tú no tienes que tirar piedras a nadie.)

Presente

(af.)   Robert and John CAST lots with their friends.
(Roberto y Juan echan suertes con sus amigos.)

(neg.)   Robert and John DO NOT CAST lots with their friends.

(int.)   DO Robert and John CAST lots with their friends?

Pasado

(af.)   The crowd CAST stones to a mad dog *yesterday.*
(La muchedumbre tiró piedras a un perro rabioso ayer.)

178

(neg.) The crowd DID NOT *cast* stones to a mad dog *yesterday*.

(int.) DID the crowd *cast* stones to a mad dog *yesterday?*

Antepresente

(af.) They *have CAST* a *glance* to that sales report.
(Ellos han echado una ojeada a ese informe de ventas.)

(neg.) They *have* NOT *CAST* a *glance* to that sales report.

(int.) *Have* they *CAST* a *glance* to that sales report?

Ejemplos ilustrativos de cómo emplear el verbo marcado con el número 2 en sus tiempos y formas fundamentales: clasificación *CAST, CAST, CAST.*

Infinitivo

They are going *to* broad*CAST* that radio show from coast to coast.
(Van a difundir esa función de radio de costa a costa.)

Presente

(af.) They broad*CAST* a transmission in Spanish *every night*.
(Ellos difunden una transmisión en español todas las noches.)

(neg.) They DO NOT broad*CAST* a transmission in Spanish *every night*.

(int.) DO they broad*CAST* a transmission in Spanish *every night?*

Pasado

(af.) They broad*CAST* a television program from coast to coast *last night*.
(Ellos difundieron un programa de televisión de costa a costa anoche.)

(neg.) They DID NOT broad*cast* a television program from coast to coast *last night*.

(int.) DID they broad*cast* a television program from coast to coast *last night?*

(af.) They *have* broad*CAST* many cultural programs on television.
(Ellos han difundido muchos programas culturales por televisión.)

(neg.) They *have* NOT broad*CAST* many cultural programs on television.

(int.) *Have* they broad*CAST* many cultural programs on television?

Ejemplos ilustrativos de cómo emplear el verbo marcado con el número 3 en sus tiempos y formas fundamentales: clasificación *CAST, CAST, CAST.*

Infinitivo

Some scientists are trying *to* fore*CAST* the weather of earth in a hundred years.
(Algunos hombres de ciencia están tratando de predecir el estado atmosférico de la tierra dentro de cien años.)

Presente

(af.) Some newspapers fore*CAST* the weather *every day.*
(Algunos periódicos predican el estado atmosférico todos los días.)

(neg.) Some newspapers DO NOT fore*CAST* the weather *every day.*

(int.) DO some newspapers fore*CAST* the weather *every day?*

Pasado·

(af.) The Weather Bureau fore*CAST* bad weather *yesterday.*
(La oficina meteorológica predijo mal tiempo ayer.)

(neg.) The Weather Bureau DID NOT fore*cast* bad weather *yesterday.*

(int.) DID the Weather Bureau fore*cast* bad weather. *yesterday?*

Antepresente

(aɪf.)   The Radio Broadcastings *have* fore*CAST* showers and
cloudy weather.
(Las raoiodifusoras han predicho aguaceros y tiempo
nublado.)

(neg.)   The Radio Broadcastings *have* NOT fore*CAST* showers
and cloudy weather.

(int.)   *Have* the Radio Broadcastings fore*CAST* showers and
cloudy weather?

LOS VERBOS REGULARES
MAS USUALES

Para complementar en forma cabal y exitosa este enfoque lingüístico para la asimilación efectiva del inglés, se da a continuación una lista de verbos esenciales en la más usual expresión cotidiana.

Como puede apreciarse, esta selección ha sido hecha tomando como base su orden alfabético en español, con traducción al inglés, a fin de facilitar la rápida localización de la acción que se desee expresar en esa lengua extranjera.

El objeto primordial de esta recopilación es que usted pueda expresar en inglés cada uno de los verbos esenciales en todas sus formas gramaticales básicas, con la ayuda, claro está, de los patrones de construcción aquí expuestos. Éstos servirán de modelo eficaz para formar cualquier tipo de oración en cualquier momento dado.

A

Abandonar, abandon
Abanicar, fan
Abarcar, comprehend
Abastecer, cater; supply; furnish; afford
Abatir, depress
Abdicar, abdicate
Ablandar, soften
Abofetear, slap
Abogar, plead
Abolir, abolish
Abordar, board
Aborrecer, detest; hate
Abotonar, button
Abrazar, embrace; hug
Abreviar, abbreviate
Abrigar, cherish
Abrigar, shelter
Abrir, open
Abrir (con llave), unlock
Abrochar, button
Abrocharse, fasten

Abrumar, overwhelm; bewilder
Absolver, absolve
Absorber, absorb
Abstenerse, abstain
Abstenerse de, refrain
Aburrir, bore
Abusar, abuse
Acalorar, excite
Acalorarse, chafe
Acanalar, corrugate
Acampar, camp
Acariciar, caress
Acariciar (moralmente), cherish
Acariciar mimar, pet
Aceitar, lubricate; oil
Acelerar, precipitate
Acentuar (palabras), accent
Acentuar, enfatizar, accentuate
Acepillar, plane
Aceptar, accept
Acercarse, approach
Acceder, accede
Aclamar, acclaim
Aclarar, clarify; clear

Aclimatar, acclimate
Acomodar, accommodate
Acompañar, accompany; escort
Aconsejar, advise; counsel
Acontecer, happen
Acordar, concert
Acortar, shorten
Acosar, harass
Acreditar, accredite
Activar, activate
Acumular, accumulate; store
Acuñar, coin
Acusar, accuse
Achacar, attribute
Adaptar, adapt
Adherir, adhere
Adivinar, guess
Adjudicar, adjudicate
Administrar, administer
Admirar, admire
Admitir, admit; concede
Adorar, adore; worship
Adornar, adorn; decorate; ornament
Adquirir, acquire
Aducir, adduce
Adular, flatter; cajole
Adulterar, adulterate
Advertir, warn; notice
Afamar, fame
Afear, desfigure
Afectar, affect
Afilar, sharpen
Afinar, tone; tune
Afirmar, affirm; assure
Afligir, afflict
Aflojar, loosen; unfasten; unloosen
Aforar, appraise
Afrontar, affront; face
Agarrar, grasp; grip; seize
Agitar, agitate
Agitar, stir
Agitarse (el mar), surge
Agolparse, crowd
Agotar, exhaust
Agradar, please
Agradecer, appreciate

Agradecer, thank
Agrandar, enlarge
Agraviar, wound
Agrietarse, crack
Agrupar, group
Aguardar, wait; expect
Agujerear, perforate
Ahogar, choke
Ahogar(se), drown
Ahondar, deepen
Ahorcar (colgando), hang
Ahorrar, save
Ahumar, fumigate
Airear, air
Ajustar, adjust
Alabar, praise
Alardear, bluff; boast
Alargar, lengthen
Alarmar, alarm
Albergar, shelter
Alcanzar, reach; attain
Alegrarse, cheer
Alegrarse, rejoice
Alentar, encourage; animate
Aletear, wing
Alfombrar, carpet
Aliar, ally
Alinear, line
Aliviar, ease
Almacenar, store
Almidonar, starch
Almorzar, lunch
Alojar, house; lodge
Alquilar, hire; rent
Alterar, alter
Alternar, alternate
Aludir, allude
Alumbrar, light
Alzar, raise; lift
Amalgamar, amalgamate
Amamantar, suckle; suck
Amanecer, dawn
Amansar, domesticate; tame
Amar, love
Amarrar, tie
Amenazar, menace
Amenazar, amagar, threaten
Aminorar, lessen

183

Amonestar, admonish
Amontonar, pile
Amortizar, redeem
Amotinarse, riot
Ampliar, ensanchar, widen
Amplificar, amplify
Amputar, amputate
Amueblar, furnish
Analizar, analyze
Anclar, anchor
Andar, walk; hike
Anexar, annex
Anhelar, long
Anhelar, yearn
Anidar, nest
Animar, animate; encourage
Aniquilar, annihilate
Antagonizar, antagonize
Anticipar, anticipate
Anudar, knot
Anular, abrogate
Anunciar, advertise
Anunciar, announce
Apadrinar, sponsor
Aparentar, pretend
Apedrear, lapidate; stone
Apelar, appeal
Apiñarse, crowd
Aplacar, appease
Aplanar, flatten
Aplastar, smash
Aplaudir, applaud; clap
Aplicar, apply
Apoyar, back
Apoyar, support; second
Apreciar, aforar, appraise
Apreciar, appreciate; esteem
Apremiar, urge
Aprender, learn
Apresurar, precipitate
Apresurar, urge
Apresurarse, hurry; hasten
Apresurarse, rush
Apretar, compress
Apretar, push; squeeze
Apretar, tighten
Aprobar, approve
Apropiarse, appropiate

Aprovechar, avail
Aproximarse, approach
Apuntar, aim
Apuntar, señalar, point
Apurarse, hurry; hasten
Aquietar, appease
Arar, furrow; plow; plough
Arar, plow; plough
Arbitrar, umpire
Archivar, file, record
Arder, kindle
Arengar, harangue
Argüir, argue
Argumentar, argue
Armar, arm
Armonizar, harmonize
Articular, articulate
Arraigarse, root
Arrancar (un carro), start
Arrasar, desolate
Arrasar, raze
Arrastrar, drag
Arrastrar, haul
Arrastrar, trail
Arrastrar, remolcar, tug
Arrastrarse, crawl
Arrebatar, snatch
Arreglar, arrange; fix
Arreglar las uñas, manicure
*Arreglar, componer, zurcir, re-
mendar*, mend
Arreglar, componer (el pelo),
trim
Arremolinarse, swirl
Arrendar, alquilar, lease; rent
Arrepentirse, arrepentirse de,
repent
Arrestar, arrest
Arribar, arrive
Arriesgarse, dare; expose
Arriesgar(se), risk
Arrinconar, corner
Arrogarse, usurp
Arrojar, vomit
Arrugar, corrugate
Arrugarse, wrinkle
Arrullar, lull
Asaltar, assault

Asar, roast
Ascender, ascend
Asear, clean
Asediar, besiege
Asegurar, assure
Asegurarse, insure
Asentir, assent
Asesinar, assessinate; murder
Asesorar, counsel
Asfaltar, asphalt
Asfixiar, asphyxiate; choke
Asignar, assign
Asimilar, assimilate
Asistir, asistir a, attend
Asociar, adjoin
Asociar(se), associate
Asolar, devastate
Asombrar, amaze; astonish
Aspirar, aspire
Asumir, assume
Asustar, frighten; scare
Atacar, attack
Atar, attach, tie
Atar, lace
Atender, attend
Atender a, mind
Atenuar, dim
Aterrar, terrify
Aterrizar, land
Aterrorizar, terrify
Atesorar, hoard
Atestiguar, witness, attest
Atisbar, peep
Atornillar, screw
Atraer attract
Atrancar (puerta), bar
Atreverse, dare
Atribuir, attribute
Atrincherar, trench
Aturdir, confuse
Aumentar, encrease; aument
Autenticar, authenticate
Autorizar, authorize; authenticate
Avanzar, advance
Aventar, ventilar, despajar, winnow
Aventurar(se), venture

Averiar, damage
Avisar, advise
Avisar, advertir, warn
Ayudar, auxiliar, help; aid; assist
Ayunar, fast
Azotar, whip; lash
Azuzar, incite

— B —

Babear, drivel
Bailar, dance
Bajar, lower
Balancear, balance
Balar, bleat
Balbucear, stammer
Bañarse, bathe
Barajar, shuffle
Barnizar, varnish
Barrenar, bore
Barrenar, drill
Batir, clash; stir
Bautizar, baptize
Bendecir, bless
Beneficiar(se), benefit
Besar, kiss
Blandir, brandish
Blanquear, bleach; whiten
Blasfemar, blaspheme
Bloquear, blockade
Bolear, shine
Bombardear, bombard
Bombear, pump
Bordar, embroider
Borrar (con goma), erase rub
Bostezar, yawn
Botar, echar al agua, launch
Boxear, box
Bramar, bellow, roar
Brillar suavemente, glow
Brincar, jump
Brindar por, brindar a la salud de, toast
Bromear, joke; jest; trifle
Brotar, gush; sprout
Bruñir, burnish
Bucear, dive

185

Bufar, snort
Buscar, search

– C –

Caber, contain
Cablegrafiar, cable
Cacarear, cackle; crow
Caerse, collapse
Calcar, calk
Calcular, calculate
Calentar, heat; warm
Calificar, qualify
Calmar, calm; soothe
Calumniar, slander
Callarse, hush
Cambiar, change
Cambiar, exchange
Cambiar, shift
Cambiar de casa, move
Caminar, walk; hike
Cancelar, cancel
Canjear, exchange
Cansar, tire
Cantar (el gallo), crow
Capitalizar, capitalize
Capitular, capitulate
Capturar, capture
Caracterizar, characterize
Carecer, lack; want
Cargar, cobrar, charge
Casar, wed
Casarse, casarse con, marry
Castigar, punish
Catalogar, catalogue
Catequizar, catechize
Causar, cause
Cauterizar, cauterize
Cautivar, captivate
Cazar, hunt; chase
Ceder, cede
Celebrar, celebrate
Censurar, censure
Centrar, centre
Cerner, sift
Certificar, certify
Cerrar, close
Cerrar (con llave), lock

Cesar, cease
Circular, circulate
Citar, cite; convene
Citar, quote
Civilizar, civilize
Clamar, exclaim
Clasificar, classify
Claudicar, limp
Clavar, nail
Coagularse, coagulate
Cobrar, cargar, charge
Cobrar (un cheque), collect; cash
Cocear, kick
Cocer, cook
Cocinar, cook
Codiciar, covet
Codiciar, envy
Coger, grasp
Coincidir, coincide
Cojear, limp
Colaborar, colaborate
Colectar, gather
Colocar, place; locate, settle
Colonizar, colonize
Colorar, color
Combatir, combat
Combinar, combine
Comentar, comment
Comenzar, commence
Comenzar, start
Comer (la comida principal). dine
Comerciar, trade; traffic
Compadecerse, pity; simpathize
Comparar, compare
Compartir, share
Compelir, compel
Compensar, compensate
Competir, compete
Complacer, please
Completar, complete
Complicar, complicate
Componer, compose
Componer, compound
Comprar, purchase
Comprender, comprehend

Comprender, comprise; conceive
Comprimir, compress; squeeze
Comprobar, prove
Comprobar, test
Comprometer, engage
Comprometerse, compromise
Computar, compute
Comunicar, communicate
Concebir, conceive
Conceder, grant; allow; concede
Concentrarse, concentrate
Concernir, concern
Concertar, concert
Concluir, conclude
Concretar, concrete
Condenar, condemn
Condenar, damn
Condensar, condense
Condescender, condescend
Condonar, condone
Conducir, conduct
Conectar, connect
Conferir, confer
Confesar, confess
Confiar, trust
Confirmar, confirm
Confiscar, confiscate
Conformarse, conform
Confortar, comfort; console
Confrontar, check
Confrontar, confront
Confundir, confuse; confound; puzzle
Congregar, congregate
Conjeturar, conjecture
Conjugar, conjugate
Conmemorar, commemorate
Conmoverse, thrill
Conquistar, conquer
Consagrar, consecrate
Consentir, consent
Conservar, conserve
Considerar, consider
Consistir, consist
Consolar, console
Consolidar, consolidate

Conspirar, conspire; plot
Constituir, constitute
Constreñir, constrain
Construir, construc
Consultar, consult
Consumar, consummate
Contagiar, infect
Contaminar, contaminate
Contar, count
Contemplar, contemplate
Contemplar, gaze
Contemporizar, temporize
Contener, comprise
Contener, contain
Contener, content
Contentar, please
Contestar, answer; reply
Continuar, continue
Contrabandear, smuggle
Contradecir, contradict
Contraer, contract
Contrariar, counteract
Contrarrestar, counteract
Contravenir, contravene
Contribuir, contribute
Controlar, control
Convalecerse, convalesce
Convencer, convince
Converger, converge
Conversar, converse
Convertir, convert
Convocar, convoke; convene
Cooperar, cooperate
Coordinar, coordinate
Copiar, copy
Coquetear, flirt
Coronar, crown
Cortar (en rebanadas), slice
Cortejar, court; escort; woo
Corregir, correct
Correr (un río), flow
Corresponder, corresponde
Corroborar, corroborate; confirm
Corromper, corrupt; deprave
Cosechar, crop; harvest; reap
Cotizar, quote
Crear, create

Crecer, sprout
Creer, believe; guess
Criar, raise
Cristalizar, crystalize
Criticar, criticize
Crujir; crackle; creak
Crucificar, crusify
Cruzar, cross
Cruzar (por mar), cruise
Cuadriplicar, quadruplicate
Cuartearse, crack
Cubrir, cover
Cuidar, mind
Culminar, culminate
Cultivar, cultivate; raise
Cumplimentar, compliment
Cumplir, fullfill
Cumplir con, comply
Curar, sanar, cure; remedy

— CH —

Chantajear, blackmail
Chapotear, splash
Charlar, platicar, chat
Chiflar, whistle
Chillar, creak; scream; shriek
Chismear, gossip
Chispear, sparkle
Chocar, shock, clash, collide
Chorrear, drip
Chulear, quiz
Chupar, sip; suck

— D —

Damnificar, damnify
Dañar, damage; harm; spoil
Dar, hand
Dar a, overlook
Dar asco, sicken
Dar forma, shape
Dar fuerza, enforce
Dar la bienvenida, welcome
Dar las gracias, thank
Dar propina, tip; fee
Dar sombra, shade
Dar un grito, utter

Dar un tirón, jerk
Dar una tunda, whale
Dar vuelta, turn
Darse cuenta, darse cuenta de
realize
Debastar, debastate
Debatir, debate
Deber, must; ought
Deber, owe
Debilitar, weaken
Debilitar(se), debilitate;
weaken
Decaer, decay
Decapitar, behead
Decepcionar, disappoint
Decidir, decide
Decir, uter
Declamar, declaim
Declarar, declare; testify;
witness
Declarar, exponer, state,
Declinar, decline
Decolorarse, fade
Decorar, decorate
Decrecer, decrease
Decretar, decree
Dedicar(se), devote
Deducir, deduce
Defecar, defecate
Defender, defend
Definir, define
Deformar, deform
Defraudar, cheat; defraude,
dissapoint
Degenerar, degenerate
Deglutir, swallow
Degradar, degrade
Dejar caer, drop
Dejar, quit
Delatar, denounce
Delatar, dilate
Delegar, delegate
Deletrear, spell
Delinear, delineate, outline
Delinear, outline
Delinear, trazar, trace
Delirar, rave
Demandar, demand

188

Demoler, demolish
Demorarse, delay
Demostrar, demonstrate; prove
Denegar, deny
Denigrar, denigrate
Denominar, denominate
Denotar, denote
Denunciar, denounce
Depender, depend
Deplorar, deplore; moan
Deponer, depose
Deportar, deport
Depositar, deposit
Depravarse, deprave
Depreciar(se), depreciate
Deprimir, depress
Depurar, depurate
Derivar, derive
Derogar, derogate; revoke
Derramar, spill
Derrapar, skid
Derretir, melt; smelt
Derrochar, waste
Derrotar, defeat
Derrumbarse, crumble
Desabotonar, unbutton
Desabrochar, unbotton;
   unfasten
Desacatar, disrespect
Desacreditar, discredit
Desafiar, challenge; defy
Desairar, slight
Desalojar, dislodge
Desalojar, remover, displace
Desanimarse, discourage
Desanudar, untie
Desaparecer, disappear
Desaprobar, disapprove
Desarmar, disarm
Desarreglar, disarrange
Desarrollar, develop
Desarrugar, unwrinkle
Desatar, loose; untie
Desatar, unfasten; unloose;
   untie; unloosen
Desatender, neglect
Desatornillar, unscrew
Desbocarse, bolt

Desbordarse, overflow
Descalificar, desqualify
Descansar, rest; relax
Descargar, unload
Descargar, discharge
Descargar, unload; unburden
Descartar, discard
Descarrilar, derail
Descascarar, peel; shell
Descender, descend
Descifrar, decipher
Descomponer, disarrange
Descomponerse, decompose
Desconcertar, disconcert;
   embarass
Desconectar, disconnect
Desconfiar, distrust
Descontar, discount
Descontinuar, discontinue
Describir, describe; depict
Descubrir, discover; uncover
Descubrir, uncover
Descubrir, publicar, utter
Descubrirse para saludar, cap
Descuidar, neglect
Desdeñar, disdain
Desdoblar, unfold
Desear, wish; desire; want
Desear, saber, wonder
Desear vivamente, yearn
Desecar, desicate
Desenvainar, unsheathe
Desembarcar, disembark; land
Desempacar, unpack
Desempolvar, dust
Desencadenar, unchain
Desencuadernar, unloose
Desengañar, undeceive
Desengañarse, undeceive
   oneself
Desenganchar, unhook;
   unfasten
Desenyugar, unyoke
Desenmascarar, unmask
Desensillar, unsaddle
Desenterrar, exhume; unbury
Desenvolver, unfold; unwrap
Desequilibrar, unbalance

Desertar, desert
Desesperarse, despair
Desfigurar, disfigure
Desfilar, parade
Desgranar, husk
Deshacer una formación, dismiss
Desheredar, disinherit
Deshidratarse, dehydrate
Deshollejar, husk
Deshonrar, dishonor
Deshonrar (a una mujer), violate
Designar, designate; nominate
Desilusionarse, disillusion
Desinfectar, disinfect
Desistir, desist
Desligar, untie
Deslindar terrenos, survey
Deslizar, skid
Deslizarse, skim; slip
Deslumbrar, dazzle
Deslustrar, tarnish
Desmantelar, dismantle
Desmayarse, faint
Desmembrar, dismember
Desmenuzar, chip; crumble
Desmontarse, dismount
Desmoralizarse, demoralize
Desnudar(se), undress
Desobedecer, disobey
Desolar, desolate
Desorganizar, disorganize
Despachar, dispatch; forward
Despajar, winnow
Despechar, destetar, wean
Despegar, detach
Desperdiciar, waste
Despertar(se), wake; waken; awake; awaken
Desplegar, display; unfold
Desplomarse, collapse
Desdoblar, depopulate
Despojar, deprive; despoil
Despolvorear, sprinkle
Despreciar, despise
Destacar, feature
Destapar, uncap

Destapar, desarropar, uncover
Desterrar, deport; banish
Destilar, distil
Destinar, destine
Destituir, fire; destitute; depose
Destorcer, untwist
Destrancar, unbar
Destrozar, destroy
Desunir, disunite
Desvariar, rave
Desvendar, undress
Desvestir(se), undress
Desviar, divert; shift
Detallar, detail
Detener, detain, stop
Detenerse, pararse, stop
Detenerse, quedarse, stay
Deteriorar(se), damage; decay deteriorate
Determinar, determine
Detestar, detest
Devaluar, devaluate
Devorar, devour
Diagnosticar, diagnose
Dibujar, sketch
Dictar, dictate
Dictar conferencias, lecture
Diezmar, decimate
Difamar, defame
Diferir, defer; differ
Diferir, diferenciar, differ
Difundir, diffuse
Dignarse, deign
Dilapidar, dilapidate; waste
Dilatarse, delay
Dirigir la palabra, address
Dirigir, direct
Dirigir, manage; direct
Dirigir mal, misdirect
Discrepar, diferir, disagree
Disculparse, apologize; excuse oneself
Discutir, discuss; debate
Disecar, dissect; stuff
Diseminar, disseminate
Diseñar, design; sketch
Disertar, lecture

190

Disfrazarse, disguise
Disfrutar, enjoy
Disgustar, dislike; disgust; shock
Disimular, dissimulate; wink
Disipar, dissipate
Dislocarse, dislocate
Disminuir, diminish
Disolver, disolve
Disolver, licenciar, dismiss
Disparar, discharge; fire
Dispensar, dispense
Dispensar, excuse
Dispersar, disperse
Disponer, dispose
Disputar, dispute
Distinguir, distinguish
Distribuir, distribute
Disuadir, disuade
Divagar, digress
Divertir, entertain
Dividir, divide
Divisar, discry
Divorciarse, divorciarse de, divorce
Doblar, duplicar, double
Doblar, fold
Documentarse, document
Domar, tame
Domesticar, domesticate
Dominar, dominate
Donar, bestow; donate
Dosificar, dose
Dotar, endow
Dramatizar, dramatize
Drenar, drain
Dudar, doubt
Dulcificar, sweeten
Duplicar, duplicate
Durar, last

— E —

Eclipsar, eclipse
Economizar, economize
Echar al agua, launch
Echar bravatas, bully
Echar clavados, dive

Echar la culpa a, blame
Echar de menos, miss
Echar raices, root
Echar un vistazo, glance
Editar, edit
Educar, educate
Efectuar, effect
Ejecutar, execute
Ejercer, ejercitar, exercise
Elaborar, elaborate
Electrificar, electrify
Electrocutar, electrocute
Elegir, elect
Elevar, elevate
Eliminar, eliminate
Eludir, elude
Emanar, emanate
Emancipar, emancipate
Embarcar, embark
Embarcar, enviar, ship
Embargar, embargo
Embarrar, plast
embarrar, smear
Embelesar, enchant
Embellecer, beautify
Emblanquecer, whiten
Embotar, blunt, enervate
Embotellar, bottle
Embravecerse (el mar), surge
Embrujar, bewitch
Embrutecerse, imbrute
Embutir, stuff
Emigrar, emigrate
Emitir, emit
Emocionarse, thrill
Empacar, pack
Empañar(se), tarnish
Empapar, drench; saturate
Emparejar, equal; equalize
Empedrar, pave
Empeñar, pawn
Empeorar, impair
Empeorarse, worsen
Empezar, start
Emplear, employ; occupy
Empobrecer, impoverish
Empolvarse, powder
Empotrar, embed

Empujar, rush; push
Empuñar, grip
Emular, emulate
Enaltecer, extol
Enamorar, woo
Encadenar, chain
Enarbolar, hoist
Encallar, strand
Encantar, charm; delight; enchant
Encapricharse, conceit
Encararse con, face
Encarcelar, jail
Encargar, entrust
Encementar, cement
Encender, light
Encerar, wax
Encolerizarse, enrage
Encomendar, commend
Encomiar, praise
Encontrar, encounter
Encubrir, conceal
Encumbrarse, soar
Encurtir, pickle
Enderezar, straighten
Endiosar, deify
Endosar, endorse; indorse
Endulzar, sweeten
Endurecer, harden; hinder
Enervar, enervate
Enfadar, vex
Enfatizar, emphasize; stress
Enfermarse, sicken
Enfrentarse a, face
Enfurecerse, madden; infurate; rage
Enganchar, hook
Engañar, cheat; deceive; fool; trick
Engañarse, fool oneself; deceive oneself
Engendrar, engender; procreate
Engomar, gum
Engordar, fatten
Engrapar, staple
Engrasar, grease; oil
Engreírse, conceit
Enguantar, glove

Engusanarse, spoil
Enhebrar, thread
Enjaular, cage; encage
Enjabonar, soap
Enjuagar, rinse
Enjugar, wipe
Enladrillar, pave
Enlatar, can
Enlazar, enlace; lace
Enlistar, enrolar, enlist; list; enroll
Enlodar, splash
Enloquecerse, madden
Enmascarar, mask
Ennegrecer, blacken, darken
Ennoblecer, ennoble
Enredar, entangle
Enredarse, embrollarse, tangle
Enriquecerse, enrich
Enrollar, wrap
Ensalzar, extol
Ensanchar, enlarge; widen
Ensartar, thread
Ensayar, rehearse
Ensillar, saddle
Ensordecer, deafen
Ensuciar, dirty; soil
Enterrar, bury
Entintar, ink
Entonar(se), intonate
Entonar, tone; tune
Entrenar, train; coach
Entrar, entrar a, enter
Entreabrir, half open
Entregar, deliver; hand
Entregarse, rendirse, surrender
Entrelazar, interlace
Entrelinear, interline
Entremeterse, intromit; intrude
Entretener, entertain
Entrevistar, interview
Entristecerse, sadden
Ennumerar, enumerate
Enunciar, enunciate
Envasar, enlatar, can; tin
Envenenar, poison
Envenenarse, emborracharse, intoxicate

Enviar, dispatch; forward
Envidiar, envy
Envolver, envelop
Envolver, wrap
Enyesar, plast
Enyugar, yoke
Equipar, equip
Erigir, erect
Eructar, belch, eruct
Erradicar, eradicate
Esbozar, sketch
Escalar, scale
Escaldar, scald
Escandalizar, scandalize
Escapar, escape
Escapar de, slip
Escarnecer, gibe
Escatimar, scant; stint
Esclavizar, enslave; slave
Esconder, conceal
Escribir en máquina, type;
    typewrite
Escribir con mayúscula,
    capitalize
Escrutar, poll
Escuchar, listen
Escudar, shield
Esculpir, carve; engrave
    sculpture
Escurrir drip
Esgrimir, wield
Esmaltar, enamel
Espaciar, space
Espantar, frighten; scare
Esparcir, scatter; sprinkle
Especializarse, specialize
Especificar, specify
Especular, speculate
Esperar, wait
Esperar (con más o menos
    seguridad), expect
Esperar (tener esperanzas),
    hope
Espinar, prick
Espiar, spy; watch
Espolear, spur
Esquiar, skii
Establecer, establish; settle

Estacionarse, park
Estafar, swindle; trick
Estallar, explode
Estampar, stamp
Estancarse, estacionarse,
    stagnate
Estañar, tin
Estatuir, chapter
Estereotipar, stereotype
Esterilizar, sterilize
Estigmatizar, stigmatize
Estimar, cherish; esteem
Estimar, calcular, estimate
Estimular, stimulate
Estipular, stipulate; specify
Estirar, lenghten
Estirar(se), stretch
Estorbar, hamper
Estornudar, sneeze
Estrangular, strangle
Estrechar, angostar, tighten
Entregar, scour; scroub; rub
Estrellarse, crash
Estremecerse, quake
Estreñir, constipate
Estropear, echar a perder, spoil
Estudiar, study
Evacuar, evacuate
Evadir, elude; evade
Evaporarse, evaporate
Evidenciar, evidence
Evitar, avoid; prevent
Evocar, evoke
Exagerar, exaggerate
Exaltar, exalt
Examinar, examine; survey
Examinar a un discípulo, quiz
Exasperar, exasperate
Excavar, excavate
Exceder, exceed
Exceptuar, except
Excitar, excite
Exclamar, exclaim
Excluir, exclude
Excomulgar, excomunicate
Excusar, excuse
Exhalar, exhale

Exhibir, exhibit
Exhortar, exhort
Exhumar, exhume; unbury
Exigir, demand
Eximir, exempt
Existir, exist
Expectorar, expectorate
Expedir, expedite
Expeler, expel
Experimentar, experience
Experimentar, experiment
Expiar, expiate
Expirar, expire
Explicar, explain
Explorar, explore
Explotar, explode
Explotar (sacar utilidad), exploit
Exponer, display
Exponer, expose
Exponer, state
Exportar, export
Expresar, express; state
Exprimir, squeeze
Expropiar, expropiate
Extender, extend
Extender, stretch
Extender, unfold
Exterminar, exterminate
Extinguirse, extinguish
Extirpar, extirpate
Extraer, extract

— F —

Fabricar, manufacture; fabricate
Facilitar, expedite; facilitate
Facturar, invoice
Falsificar, counterfeit; falsify
Faltar, lack
Faltar al respeto, disrespect
Fallar, fail
Fallecer, decease
Fanfarronear, brag; boast
Fantasear, fancy
Fascinar, fascinate; bewitch

Fastidiar, annoy; bother; tease
Fatigarse, fatigue; tire
Favorecer, favor
Fecundar, fecund
Fechar, date
Felicitar, congratulate
Fermentar, ferment
Fertilizar, fertilize
Figurarse, figure
Fijar, fix
Filtrar, filter
Fingir, simulate
Firmar, sign
Flagelar, whip
Flamear, wave
Flanquear, flank
Florecer, bloom; flourish
Flotar, float
Fluctuar, fluctuate
Foliar, folio
Fomentar, foment; foster
Forjar, forge
Formar, form
Formar, dar forma, shape
Formular, formulate
Fortalecer, strenghten
Fortificar, fortify
Forzar, force
Forzar la vista, strain
Fotografiar, photograph
Fracasar, fail
Fracturar(se), fracture
Franquear, frank
Frecuentar, frequent
Fregar, estregar, scour; scrub
Freir, fry
Frotar, rub; wipe
Fruncir el ceño, frown; scowl; wrinkle
Frustrar, disappoint; frustrate
Fumar, smoke
Fumigar, fumigate
Funcionar, function
Fundar, found
Fundir, melt; smelt
Fundirse, fuse
Fustiga, fustigate; whip

194

– G –

Galantear, compliment; court; woo
Galopar, gallop
Galvanizar, galvanize
Ganar, gain
Ganar (dinero), earn
Garantizar, guarantee
Gemir, wail
Generalizar, generalize
Germinar, germinate
Girar, revolve
Glorificar, glorify
Gobernar, govern; rule; rein
Golpear, clash; knock
Gorjear, trill; warble
Gotear, leak; drip
Gozar, enjoy
Grabar, engrave; grave
Grabar (en cinta o disco), record
Graduar, ordenar, grade
Graduarse, graduate
Granizar, hail
Granular, granulate
Gratificar, gratify
Gravar, burden
Gravitar, gravitate
Graznar, croak
Gritar, cry; shout
Gritar, chillar, scream
Gruñir, groan; growl; grunt
Guardar, ward
Guardar silencio, hush
Guarnecer, harness; garrison
Guerrear, war
Guiar, guide
Guiñar, blink; wink
Gustar, querer, like
Gustar (al paladar), taste

– H –

Habérselas con, face
Habitar, inhabit
Hablar entre dientes, mutter
Hacer caso de, mind
Hacer cosquillas, tickle
Hacer efectivo un cheque, letra, etc., cash
Hacer erupción, erupt
Hacer falta, miss
Hacer fuerza, strain
Hacer germinar, sprout
Hacer juego con, match
Hacer malla, knit
Hacer pedazos, smash
Hacer señar, hacer señales, wave
Hacer zanjas, trench
Hacerse de la vista gorda, wink
Haraganear, idle; loaf
Hartarse, glut; stuff
Heredar, inherit
Herir, wound
Herir con arma blanca, stab
Hervir, boil
Hipnotizar, hypnotize
Hipotecar, mortgage
Honrar, honor
Hormiguear, swarm
Hornear, bake
Horrorizarse, horrify
Hospedar, lodge
Hospedarse, stay
Hostigar, vex
Humanizar, humanize
Humedecer, damp; dampen; moisten
Humillar(se), humble
Hundirse, immerge
Hurgar, stir
Husmear, sniff

– I –

Idealizar, idealize
Idear, inventar, ingeniar. contrive
Identificar, identify
Idolatrar, idolize
Ignorar, ignore
Igualar, equalize
Iluminar, illuminate; light; lighten

Ilustrar, illustrate
Imaginarse, imagine
Imanar, magnetize
Imitar, imitate; mimic
Impartir, impart
Impedir, impede; hinder; prevent
Impeler, impel
Implicar, imply
Implorar, implore; plead
Imponer, impose
Imponer pena o castigo, penalize
Importar, import
Importar, concern
Importarle a uno, care
Importunar, importune
Imposibilitar, disable
Impregnar, impregnate
Impresionar, impress
Imprimir, imprint; print
Imprimir con errores, misprint
Improvisar, improvize
Inaugurar, inaugurate
Incendiar, fire
Incinerar, incinerate
Incitar, incite; tempt
Inclinarse, incline; lean; sway
Incluir, include, embody
Incluir, acompañar, remitir, enclose
Incomodarse, incomode
Incorporarse, incorporate
Incriminar, incriminate
Incubar, incubate, hatch
Inculcar, inculcate
Indemnizar, indemnify
Indicar, indicate
Inducir, induce
Industrializar, industrialize
Infatuar, infatuate
Infectar, infect
Inferir, infer
Infestar, infest
Infiltrarse, infiltrate
Inflamar, hinchar, inflate
Inflamarse, inflame
Infligir, inflict

Influir, influence
Informar, inform; report; advise
Infrigir. infringe; violate; transgress
Infundir, infuse
Inhabilitar, disable
Inhalar, inhale
Inhumar, bury
Iniciar, initiate
Injertar, graft, engraft
Injuriar, outrage
Inmigrar, immigrate
Inmovilizar, immobilize
Inmunizar, inmunize
Innovar, innovate
Inocular, inoculate
Inquietar, disquiet
Inquirir, inquire
Inscribir, inscribe; register
Insertar, insert
Insinuar, insinuate
Insistir, insist
Inspeccionar, inspect; survey
Inspirar(se), inspire
Instalar, install
Instigar, instigate
Instituir, institute
Instruir, entrenar, instruct
Insuflar, insufflate
Integrar, integrate
Intentar, intend; endeavor; tru
Intensificar, intensify
Interceder, intercede
Interesar(se), interest
Interferir, inmiscuirse, interfere
Internar, intern
Interponer, interpose
Intepretar, interpret
Intervenir, intervene
Interrogar, question; interrogate
Interrumpir, disturb; interrupt
Intimidar, intimidate
Intitular, entitle
Intoxicarse, emborracharse, intoxicate
Intranquilizar, disquiet

Intrigar, intrigue
Introducir, *presentar*, introduce
Inundar, flood; inundate
Invadir, invade
Inventar, invent
Invertir, *volver al revés*, invert
Invertir (dinero), invest
Investigar, investigate; search; research
Invitar, invite
Invocar, invoke
Inyectar, inject
Irse, depart
Irradiar, radiate; eradiate
Irrigar, irrigate
Irritar, vex; irritate
Izar, hoist

— J —

Jactarse, brag
Jadear, pant
Jalar, pull
Jubilarse, retire
Jugar, play
Jugar (dinero), gamble
Juntar, *unir*, joint; adjoint; gather; unite, assemble
Justificar, justify
Juzgar, judge
Juzgar mal, misjudge

— L —

Labrar, carve
Lactar, lactate
Ladrar, bark
Lamentar(se), lament; complain; mourn; moan; regret
Lamer, lick
Lanzar, flip
Lanzar, launch
Lapidar, lapidate
Lastimar, wound
Latir, palpitate
Lavar, wash
Laxar, loose

Lazar, lasso
Legalizar, legalize
Legislar, legislate
Lesionar, wound
Levantar, lift; raise
Liar, tie
Libar, sip; suck
Libertar, free; liberate; emancipate
Librar, liberate
Licenciar, dismiss
Licuar, liquefy
Lijar, sandpaper
Limar, lime
Limitar, limit
Limpiar, clean
Limpiar frotando, wipe
Linchar, lynch
Liquidar, liquidate
Litigar, litigate
Litografiar, litograph
Lograr, attain
Lubricar, lubricate
Luchar, struggle
Luchar, *luchar con*, *forcejear*, wrestle
Lustrar, polish; shine

— LL —

Llagar, wound
Llamar, call; recall
Llegar, *arribar*, arrive
Llegar, *llegar a*, reach
Llenar, fill
Llevar cargando, carry
Llevar, *transportar*, convey
Llorar, cry
Llover, rain
Lloviznar, drizzle

— M —

Machacar, crush; pound
Madurar, ripen
Magnetizar, magnetize
Maldecir, curse; damn
Malgastar, waste

197

Maltratar, ill-treat; outrage
Manar, flow
Manchar stain
Mandar, command
Manejar, handle
Manejar, dirigir, administrar,
  manage
Manifestar, manifest
Maniobrar, maneuvre
Manipular, manipulate
Manotear, smack
Mantener, maintain; sustain
Manufacturar, manufacture
Marcar, brand; check; label;
  mark
Marcar, señalar, mark
Marcar (en deportes), score
Marchar, march
Marcharse, depart
Marchitarse, fade
Martillar, hammer
Masajear, massage
Mascar, masticate
Masticar, masticate
Masticar, rumiar, chew
Matar, kill
Matar de hambre, starve
Matricular, enlist; matriculate
Maullar, miar; mew
Mecerse, rock
Medir, measure
Meditar, meditate
Mejorar, better
Mencionar, mention
Mendigar, beg
Menear, stir
Menguar, dwindle
Menospreciar, despise
Merecer, deserve
Mezclar, mix
Militar, militate
Mirar, mirarse, look
Mirar con ira o ceño, glower;
  scowl
Mirar fijamente, stare
Mitigar, mitigate, temper; ease
Modelar, moldear, model
Moderarse, moderate; temper

Modernizar, modernize
Modificar, modify
Mofarse, mock
Moler, grind
Molestar, bother, annoy;
  tease; vex
Molestarse, trouble oneself
Mondar, pelar, shell
Monopolizar, monopolize
Morir, die; decease
Morir de hambre, starve
Mostrar, display
Mortificar, mortify
Mover(se), move
Movilizar, mobilize
Mudar las plumas las aves,
  moult
multar, fine
Multiplicar(se), multiply
Murmurar, murmur
Murmurar, gossip
Murmurar, cuchichear, whisper
Murmurar (un arroyo), warble

— N —

Nacionalizar(se), nationalize
Narrar, narrate
Naturalizarse, naturalize
Naufragar, wreck
Navegar, sail; navegate; voyage
Necesitar, need; necessitate;
  lack; require; want
Negar, deny
Negociar, negotiate
Negociar, trade; traffic;
  transact
Neutralizar, neutralize
Nombrad, name; nominate;
  appoint
No quedar bien (prendas de
  vestir), misfit
Normalizar, normalize;
  standardize
Notar, note
Notar, advertir, mirar, notice
Notificar, notify

198

Numerar, number
Nutrir, nourish

— O —

Obedecer, obey
Objetar, oponerse, object
Obligar, oblige
Oscurecer, blacken; darken; dim
Observar, observe; watch
Obstruir, obstruct
Obtener, obtain
Ocupar, occuppy
Ocurrir, occur
Ofender, offend; harm; wound
Oficiar, officiate
Ofrecer, offer
Omitir, omit
Ondear, undulate; wave
Ondular, undulate
Ondular el cabello, wave
Operar, operate
Oponer, oppose
Oprimir, oppress
Orar, pray
Ordenar, order; command
Ordeñar, milk
Organizar, organize
Originar, originate
Qscilar, oscillate
Otorgar, grant
Oxidar, oxidize
Oxigenar, oxygenate

— P —

Pacer, graze
Pacificar, pacify
Padecer, suffer
Palidecer, fade
Palidecer, perder el color, pale
palpar, touch
Palpitar, palpitate
Paralizar(se), paralize
Pararse, detenerse, stop
Parecer, seem

Parpadear, twinkle; wink; blink
Participar, participate
Partir, part; start
Pasar, pass; elapse
Pasar por alto, overpass
Pasearse, stroll
Pasmar, astonish
astar, graze, pasture
Pasteurizar, pasteurize
Pastorear, pasture
Patear, kick
Patentar, patent
Patinar, skate
Patinar (una rueda), skid
Patrocinar, patronize
Patrullar, patrol
Pavimentar, pave
Pecar, sin
Pedir, ask; request
Pedir prestado, borrow
Pedir, ordenar, order
Pegar, knock
Pegar con cola, glue
Peinar, comb
Peinarse, comb one's hair
Pelar, desplumar, pluck
Pelar(se), peel; shell
Pelear, quarrel; combat
Pellizcar pinch
Penetrar, penetrate
Pensionar, pension
Percibir, perceive
Perder, miss
Perdonar, condonar, condone
Perdonar, pardon
Perecer, perish
Perfeccionar, perfect
Perjorar, perforate
Perfumar(se), perfume
Perifonear, broadcast
Perjudicar. harm; impair
Permanecer, remain; stay
Permitir, permit; allow
Permutar, barter; interchange
Perpetrar, perpetrate
Perpetuar, perpetuate

Perseguir, persecute; chase; persue
Perseverar, persevere
Persistir, persist
Personificar, personalize
Persuadir, persuade
Pertenecer, belong
Perturbar, disturb
Pervertir, pervert
Pesar, weigh
Petrificar(se), petrify
Picar, itch
Picar con espuelas, spur
Picotear, picar, peck
Pintar, paint
Pintar, describir, imaginarse, picture
Pisar, step
Pitar, whistle
Plagiar, plagiarize
Planchar, press; iron
Planear, pensar, plan
Plantar, plant
Platicar, talk; chat
Poblar, populate
Podar, prune
Poner en libertad, release
Poner en peligro, imperil
Poner en vigor, enforce
Poner la dirección, address
Poner la rayita a la t, cross the t
Poner punto a la i, dot the i
Popularizar, popularize
Portarse, behave
Portarse mal, misbehave
Poseer, possess; own
Posponer, postpone
Postrarse, prosternarse, prostrate
Postular, postulate
Practicar, practice; exercise
Preceder, precede
Precipitarse, rush; precipitate
Predecir, pronosticate; predict
Predicar, preach
Predicar, proclamar, predicate; sermonize

Preferir, prefer
Preguntar, ask; question
Preguntarse, desear saber, wonder
Premeditar, premeditate
Premiar, reward
Prensar, exprimir, press
Preocuparse, worry
Preparar, prepare
Prescribir, prescribe
Presentar, present; introduce
Presenciar, witness
Presentar, exhibir, exhibit; display
Presentar, someter, subject; submit
Preservar, preserve
Presidir, preside
Presionar, presure
Prestar, loan
Presumir, aparentar, pretender, pretend
Presumir, suponer, presume
Presuponer, presuppose
Pretender, aparentar, pretend
Prevalecer, prevail
Prevenir, evitar, impedir, prevent
Prevenir, warn
Principiar, start
Probar, comprobar, demostrar, prove
Probar, intentar, try
Proceder, proceed
Proclamar, proclaim
Procrear, procreate; engender
Procurar, procure
Producir, produce; yield; generate
Profanar, profane
Profesar, profess
Profetizar, prophesy
Progresar, progress; improve
Prohibir, prohibit
Prolongar, prolong
Prometer, promise
Promover, fomentar, promote
Promulgar, promulgate; issue

Pronosticar, prognosticate
Pronunciar, pronounce
Propagar, propagate
Propender, tend
Propiciar, propitiate
Proponer(se), propose; aim
Proporcionar, furnish; provide;
  supply
Proscribir, proscribe
Proseguir, proceed; prosecute
Proseguir, pursue
Prosperar, prosper; flourish
Prostituir, prostitute
Proteger, protect
Protestar, declarar, protest
Proveer, provide; cater; supply;
  store
Provocar, provoke
Proyectar, trazar, project
Publicar, publish; issue
Pudrirse, rot; decompose
Pulir, shine; burnish
Pulverizar, pulverize
Puntear, perforar, puncture
Punzar, picar, pinchar, espinar,
  prick
Purgar, purge
Purgar, expiar, expiate
Purificar, purify

— Q —

Quebrar, crash; smash
Quebrantar, transgress
Quedarse, remain; stay
Quedarle a uno (una prenda
  de vestir), fit
Quejarse, complain
Quejarse, regret; lament
Quemar, burn; flame; scald;
  tan
Querer, desear, want; wish
Querer (de simpatía), like
Quitar, remove

— R —

Rabiar, rage

Racionar, ration
Radiar, broadcast
Radicarse, radicate
Raer, scratch; scrape
Rajar, cortar, slice
Rajarse, crack
Rallar, grate
Ramificarse, sprout
Rasar, skim
Rascar, scrape
Rasgar, rip
Rasguñar, scratch
Raspar, scratch
Rastrear, trail
Rastrillar, rake
Ratificar, ratify
Rayar, trazar, line
Razonar, reason
Reaccionar, react
Realizar, accomplish; realize
Realzar, enhance
Reanudar, resume
Reaparecer, reappear
Rebajar, underrate
Rebasar, overpass
Rebelarse, rebel; revolt
Rebotar, rebound
Rebuznar bray
Recalcar, accentuate;
  emphasize
Recalentar, rehat
Recargarse, lean
Recaudar, gather
Recibir, receive
Recibir, dar la bienvenida,
  welcome
Reclinarse, recline, lean
Reciprocar, recite
Recitar, recite
Reclamar, reclaim; claim
Reclutar, recruit
Recobrar, recover
Recoger, levantar, pick
Recoger, gather
Recomendar, recommend;
  commend
Recompensar, reward;
  recompense

Reconciliar, reconcile
Reconocer, recognize; acknowledge
Reconquistar, reconquer
Reconsiderar, reconsider
Reconstruir, reconstruct
Recopilar, digest
Recordar, remember; remind; recall
Recostarse; recline; lean
Recrear(se), recreate
Rectificar, rectify
Recuperar, recobrar la salud, reponerse, recuperate; recover
Rechazar, rehusar, refuse, reject
Redactar, redact
Redimir, amortizar, redeem
Reditar, yield
Redoblar, redouble
Reducir, reduce
Redundar, redounde
Reelegir, reelect
Reembolsar, reimburse
Reemplazar, replace
Reestablecer, reestablish
Referir, refer
Refinar, refine
Reflejar, reflect
Reflexionar, reflect
Reformar(se), reform
Reforzar, reenforce; reinforce
Refrenarse, refrain
Refrendar, authorize; vise
Refrescar, refresh; cool
Refrigerar, refrigerate
Refunfuñar, mutter
Refutar, refute
Regañar, scold
Regar, esparcir sprinkle
Regar, irrigate; water
Regatear, bargain; haggle
Regenerar, regenerate
Registrar, grabar, archivar, record
Regocijarse, rejoice
Regresar, return
Regularizar, regulate

Rehusar, refuse; decline
Reimprimir, reprint
Reinar, reigh
Reingresar, reenter
Reintegrar, reembolsar, reimburse
Reintegrar, reintegrate
Reir, laugh
Reir entre dientes, chuckle; titter
Reiterar, reiterate
Rejuvenecer, rejuvenate
Relampaguear, lighten; flash
Relatar, narrate; relate
Relegar, relegate
Relevar, release
Relinchar, neigh
Relucir, glow; glitter; shine
Rellenar, stuff; refill
Remachar, rivet
Remar, row; paddle
Remedar, mimic
Remediar, remedy; relieve
Remendar, darn; mend
Remitir, remit; enclose; forward
Remolcar, tow; trail; tug
Remontarse, soar.
Remover, remove
Remunerar, remunerate
Rendirse, surrender
Renovar, renovate; renew
Renquear, limp
Renunciar, resign; renounce
Reñir, quarrel
Reorganizar, reorganize
Reparar, repair
Repartir, share
Repasar, review
Repatriar, repatriate
Repeler, repel
Repercutir, resound; rebound; sound
Repetir, repeat
Reponer, replace
Reponerse, recover
Reposar, repose
Reprender, scold

Representar, represent; perform
Representar, simbolizar, typify
Reprimir, repress, restrain
Reprobar un examen, flunk
Reprochar, reproach
Reproducir, reproduce
Repulsar, repulse
Requerir, require
Rescatar, rescue
Rescatar, redimir, ransom
Resentirse, resent
Reservar, reserve
Residir, reside
Resignarse, resign; oneself; resign
Resistir, resist
Resolver, solucionar, solve
Resolverse, tomar un acuerdo, resolve
Resonar, resound; resonate
Resoplar, bufar, snort
Respaldar, back
Respetar, respect
Respirar, breathe; respire
Resplandecer, relucir, relumbrar, glare; glitter; sparkle
Responder, reply; answer; respond
Restablecerse, recover
Restar, subtract
Restaurar, restore
Restregar, rub
Restringir, restrict, stint
Resucitar, resuscitate
Resultar, result
Resumir, resume
Resurgir, resurge
Retardar, retard
Retener, retain
Retirarse, retire
Retocar, retouch
Retoñar, sprout
Retozar, frolic
Retractarse, retract
Retrasar, retard
Retroceder, retrocede; revert
Retumbar, thunder; rumble

Reunir, gather; reunite
Reverenciar, reverence
Revisar, revise
Revivir, revive
Revocar, derogar, revoke
Revolucionar, revolutionalize
Rezar, pray
Ridiculizar, ridicule
Rifar, raffle
Rimar, verse
Rivalizar, rival
Rizar, curl
Robar, rob
Robustecer, streghten
Rociar, salpicar, splash; drizzle
Rodar, roll
Rodear, surround
Roer, gnaw
Rogar, beg; request; ask
Romper, smash
Roncar, snore
Rotular, label
Ruborizarse, blush
Rugir, roar
Rumiar, ruminate
Rutilar, sparkle; twinkle

— S —

Saber, learn
Sabotear, sabotage
Sacar llave, unlock
Sacar punta, sharpen
Sacrificar, sacrify
Sacudir, dust
Sacudir, zarandear, jerk
Salar, salt
Salir mal en un examen, flunk
Salpicar, splash; sprinkle; • drizzle
Saltar, jump; leap; frisk; skip
Saludar, greet
Saludar (con inclinación de cabeza), bow
Sanar, heal
Saquear, pillage
Satisfacer, satisfy
Saturar, saturate

Sazonar, season
Sazonar, madurar, ripen
Secar(se), dry
Secar, enjuagar, frotar, wipe
Secuestrar, kidnap
Seducir, seduce; entice
Segar, crop
Segregar, separar, segregate
Seguir, follow; proceed
Seguir el rastro o la pista, trail
Seleccionar, select
Sellar, seal
Sembrar, sow; plant
Sentar, seat
Sentar, venir bien, suit
Sentenciar, condenar, sentence
Señalar, point
Señalar, marcar, mark
Separar, separate; detach
Separar con guión, hyphenate
Separuse, partir, part
Sepultar, bury
Ser ejemplo de, typify
Sermonear, predicar, sermonize
Servir, servir a, serve
Servir de escarmiento, warn
Significar, denotar, signify
Simbolizar, symbolize
Simpatizar, compadecer,
  sympathize
Simplificar, simplify
Simular, simulate
Sindicalizarse, syndicate
Sisear, hiss
Sitiar, besiege
Sobar, massage
Sobornar, brise
Sobrepasar, surpass
Sobrepujar, surpass
Sobresalir, feature
Sobrevenir, supervene
Sobrevivir, survive
Socabar, undermine
Socorrer, assist
Sofisticar, sofisticate
Sofocar, suffocate
Sojuzgar, subjugate; subdue;
  subject

Soldar, weld; solder
Solemnizar, solemnize
Solicitar, solicit; request; ask
Soltar, loose; loosen; untie
Soltar, poner en libertad,
  release
Soltarse, slip
Sollozar, sob
Sombrear, dar sombra, shade
Someter, presentar, subject;
  submit
Sonar, resonar, sound; jingle
Sonar produciendo tictac, tick
Sonreir(se), smile
Sonrojarse, blush
Soñar, dream
Soportar, endure
Sorber, sip
Sorprender(se), surprise
Sospechar, suspect
Sostener, mantener, sustain;
  mantain
Suavizar, smooth
Subir, climb
Sublevarse, rebel; revolt
Sublimar, exaltar, sublime
Subordinar, subordinate
Subrayar, underline
Subsistir, subsist; exist
Substraer, restar, substract
Subvencionar, subsidize
Subyugar, subdue; subjugate
Suceder, happen
Sucumbir, succumb
Sudar, perspire; transpire
Sufrir, suffer; endure
Sugerir, suggest; hint
Sujetar, sojuzgar, subject
Sumergir(se), submerge;
  inmerge; plunge
Suministrar, furnish
Superar, surpass
Supervisar, supervise
Suplantar, supplant
Suplicar, plead; request; beg
Suponer, suppose; guess;
  presume
Suprimir, suppress

Supurar, suppurate
Surtir, supply; cater; furnish;
  asort
Suscribir, subscribe
Suspender, suspend
Suspirar, sigh
Suspirar, anhelar, long (for)
Sustituir, substitute
Susurrar, whisper

— T —

Taladrar, drill; pierce
Tallar, carve
Tambalear, totter; stagger
Tapar, cover
Tapizar, upholster
Tararear, hum
Tartamudear, stammer
Tasar, appraise; rate
Tatuar, tatoo
Tejer, knit
Telefonear, phone; telephone
Telegrafiar, telegraph
Temblar, tremble; quake;
  totter; quiver; shiver
Temer, fear
Tender, propender, tend
Tener éxito, succeed
Tentar, tempt; entice
Teñir, dye
Terminar, finish; end
Testificar, declarar, testify;
  witness
Timar, swindle
Timonear, pilot
Tiranizar, tyranize
Tirar, arrojar, pitch
Tirar de, hawl; pull; tug
Tirar, jalar, drag
Tiritar, shiver; quiver
Titilar, twinkle; scintillate
Titubear, hesitate; stagger
Titular, entitle; title
Tocar, tentar, palpar, touch
Tocar, knock
Tocar un instrumento, play
Tolerar, tolerate

Torcer, twist
Tornear, turn
Torpedear, torpedo
Toser, cough
Tostar, roast; toast
Tostar, curtir, quemar, tan
Totalizar, totalize
Trabajar, work
Traducir, translate
Traer, fetch
Traficar, traffic; deal; trade
Tragar, swallow
Traicionar, betray
Trampear, swindle
Transbordar, tranfer
Transcribir, transcribe
Transcurrir, elapse
Transferir, trasladar, transfer
Transfigurar, transfigure
Transformar, transform
Transgredir, trangress
Transmitir, transmit
Transmutar, transmute
Transpirar, sudar, transpire
Trasplantar, trasplant
Transportar, transport; convey;
  carry
Trascender, trascend
Trasladar(se), move; transfer
Traslapar, overlap
Traspasar, trespass
Tratar, probar, intentar, try
Tratar, treat
Tratar, atender (a los enfer-
  mos), treat
Trazar, trace; line
Tremolar, wave
Trepar, climb
Trillar, thresh
Trinar, trill
Triplicar, triplicate
Triturar, triturate
Triunfar, succeed; triumph
Tronar, thunder
Tropezar, stumble
Trotar, trot
Truncar, truncate

Tumbar, tumble
Turbar, embarrass

— U —

Unificar, unify
Uniformar, standardize; make uniform
Unir, unite
Untar, smear

— V —

Vacar, vacate
Vaciar, empty
Vacilar, vacillate; hesitate; totter
Vacunar, vaccinate
Vadear, wade; ford
Vagar; wander; roam; stroll
Valuar, valorar, value; price; rate
Vapulear, whale
Vegetar, vegetate
Vejar, vex
Velar un muerto; wake
Vencer, dominar, master
Vencer, vanquish
Vendar, bandage
Vender al menudeo, al detalle, retail
Vender al por mayor, wholesale
Venerar, venerate
Venirle bien a uno una prenda de vestir, fit; suit
Ventilar, ventilate; window
Verificar, justificar, verify
Verse, mirarse, look
Versificar, verse
Verter, spill; pour
Vestir(se), dress

Vetar, veto
Viajar, travel
Viajar, por mar, navegar, voyage; cruise
Vibrar, vibrate
Viciar, vitiate
Victimar, victimize
Vigilar, watch
Vigorizar, invigorate
Vindicarse, vengarse, vindicate
Violar, infringir, violate
Violar, deshonrar a una mujer, violate
Visitar, visit
Vitalizar, vitalize
Vituperar, vituperate
Vivir, live
Vocalizar, vocalize
Vocear, shout
Vociferar, vociferate; shout
Volar, revolotear, wing
Volcar, overturn
Volver, return
Vomitar, vomit
Votar, votar por, vote
Votar, poll
Vulcanizar, vulcanize
Vulgarizar, vulgarize

— Z —

Zafarse, slip
Zambullirse, dive; plunch
Zanjar, ditch
Zigzaguear, zigzag
Zozobrar, capsize; wreck
Zumbir, huz; hum
Zurcar, furrow
Zurcir, darn
Zurrar, whip; tan

EJERCICIOS

Primer Grupo

Clasificación: OUGHT

Ejercicio 1. Rellene los huecos con la forma correcta del verbo en paréntesis.

1. John wants _____ _____ a new TV set. (buy)
2. He _____ his sister to the party last Friday. (bring)
3. I _____ _____ about him a lot lately. (think)
4. He came _____ _____ my advice. (seek)
5. They _____ a lot when they were married. (fight)
6. _____ you _____ groceries yesterday? (buy)
7. The Bible says "_____ and you will find." (seek)
8. My uncle _____ in Vietnam. (fight)
9. I'm sorry. I forgot _____ _____ you the book. (bring)
10. _____ you _____ it's true? (think)

Ejercicio 2. Responda a las preguntas con una frase completa.

1. Did Alison buy a new car?
   Yes, she _____.
2. Have you bought her a present?
   No, I _____.
3. Did he fight in the war?
   No, he _____.
4. Did she seek some advice?
   Yes, she _____.
5. Have you brought me that book?
   Yes, I _____.
6. Did John bring his friend to the party?
   Yes, he _____.
7. Have you thought about it?
   No, I _____.

8. Did he think of her yesterday?

   Yes, he _____.

Ejercicio 3. Lea las respuestas y escriba las preguntas.

1. No, when I was young, I did not fight a lot with my brother.

   _____?

2. Yes, John and Alice fight constantly.

   _____?

3. Yes, I buy the newspaper every day.

   _____?

4. Yes, I have bought her a birthday present.

   _____?

5. Yes, they brought many presents when they came.

   _____?

6. No, I haven't brought the book for you.

   _____?

7. Yes, I think it's a good idea.

   _____?

8. Yes, I have thought about him a lot lately.

   _____?

Clasificación: EE o EA, E-T

Ejercicio 1. Rellene los huecos con la forma correcta del verbo en paréntesis.

1. He _____ very little last night. (sleep)
2. I don't like _____ _____ my money in a bank account. (keep)
3. _____ you _____ the floor lately? (sweep)
4. She _____ when she heard the news. (weep)
5. Have you _____ the receipt? (keep)
6. We _____ each other last year. (meet)
7. I _____ _____ a little depressed lately. (feel)
8. They _____ yesterday without saying good-bye. (leave)
9. I usually _____ eight hours a day. (sleep)
10. _____ you ever _____ my brother? (meet)

Ejercicio 2. Responda a las preguntas con una frase completa.

1. Did you sleep well last night?
   No, I _____.

2. Did he keep the book?
   Yes, he _____.

3. Have they swept the floor?
   No, they _____.

4. Have you met my sister?
   No, I _____.

5. Did they leave after the concert?
   Yes, they _____.

6. Have you kept in contact?
   No, we _____.

7. Did you feel happy when you saw him?
   Yes, I _____.

8. Did she kneel during mass?
   Yes, she _____.

Ejercicio 3. Lea las respuestas y escriba las preguntas.

1. Yes, he slept on the sofa last night.
   _____?

2. No, they didn't meet in Mexico.
   _____?

3. Yes, they have left.
   _____?

4. Yes, I swept the floor yesterday.
   _____?

5. Yes, my mother wept at her brother's funeral.
   _____?

6. No, I didn't feel very tired last night.
   _____?

7. No, my cat has not often crept up on me.
   _____?

8. Yes, I have always slept with the window open.
   _____?

9. Yes, the little boy knelt before the queen.

_____?

10. Yes, we meet for coffee every morning.

_____?

Clasificación: EE o EA, E-T

Ejercicio 1. Rellene los huecos con la forma correcta del verbo en paréntesis.

1. He _____ with clients every day. (deal)
2. I _____ never _____ with such a rude person. (deal)
3. When the alarm rang, I _____ out of bed this morning. (leap)
4. People _____ in caves during the Stone Age. (dwell)
5. She often _____ to conclusions. (leap)
6. He _____ to call her yesterday. (mean)
7. I _____ _____ to call you for a long time. (mean)
8. My cat likes _____ _____ around the room. (leap)

Ejercicio 2. Responda a las preguntas con una frase completa.

1. Have you ever dealt with him?
   No, I _____.
2. Did Susan mean what she said?
   Yes, she _____.
3. Does your cat always leap around the room?
   No, my cat _____.
4. Did primitive man dwell in caves?
   Yes, primitive man _____.
5. Do you deal with a lot of customers?
   Yes, I _____.
6. Did the dolphins leap through the hoops?
   Yes, the dolphins _____.

Ejercicio 3. Lea las respuestas y escriba las preguntas.

1. No, modern man does not dwell in caves.

_____?

2. Yes, John always means what he says.

_____?

3. Yes, the dog leapt at me.

   _____?

4. No, she didn't mean to offend him.

   _____?

5. Yes, Mary has dealt with many important clients.

   _____?

6. Yes, the cat has leapt onto the sofa.

   _____?

Clasificación: D, T

Ejercicio 1. Rellene los huecos con la forma correcta del verbo en paréntesis.
1. We _____ you the merchandise last week. (send)
2. He _____ _____ a lot of money on clothes lately. (spend)
3. I don't like _____ _____ my books. (lend)
4. My parents _____ me some money last month. (lend)
5. They _____ the new train station last year. (build)
6. She _____ the letter yesterday. (send)
7. They want _____ _____ a garage behind the house. (build)
8. They _____ a lot of time together last year. (spend)

Ejercicio 2. Responda a las preguntas con una frase completa.
1. Did you send off the package?
   Yes, I _____.
2. Have they built a new airport?
   No, they _____.
3. Does John spend a lot of money on books?
   Yes, he _____.
4. Have they spent all the money?
   No, they _____.
5. Did your father build that house?
   Yes, he _____.
6. Do you send a lot of e-mails?
   No, I _____.
7. Did your parents lend you the money?
   No, they _____.

8. Did John lend you his car?

   Yes, he _____.

Ejercicio 3. Lea las respuestas y escriba las preguntas.

1. No, I did not lend John that book.

   _____?

2. Yes, I spent a lot of time on that project.

   _____?

3. Yes, they have built a new museum.

   _____?

4. Yes, she bent down to kiss the child.

   _____?

5. Yes, Susan sent me an e-mail last week.

   _____?

6. No, they do not want to build a new park.

   _____?

7. Yes, Mary always lends her sister money.

   _____?

8. No, Tom has not spent a lot of money lately.

   _____?

Clasificación: I, U

Ejercicio 1. Rellene los huecos con la forma correcta del verbo en paréntesis.

1. That washing machine _____ clothes automatically. (wring)
2. She _____ _____ the clothes out to dry. (hang)
3. Puppies often _____ to their mothers. (cling)
4. The little girl _____ to her father when the storm began. (cling)
5. I don't think a bee _____ ever _____ me. (sting)
6. The mosquitoes _____ her a lot last night. (sting)
7. John _____ the posters on the wall yesterday. (stick)
8. Peter likes _____ _____ the piano keys hard. (strike)

Ejercicio 2. Responda a las preguntas con una frase completa.

1. Did the washing machine wring the clothes?
   Yes, it _____.

2. Has John hung the painting?
   No, he _____.

3. Did the mosquitoes sting you last night?
   No, they _____.

4. Did the puppy cling to its mother?
   Yes, it _____.

5. Has a bee ever stung you?
   Yes, a bee _____.

6. Did Ann stick the labels on the folders?
   Yes, she _____.

7. Did he strike a match to light the fire?
   Yes, he _____.

8. Did he hang up on you?
   Yes, he _____.

Ejercicio 3. Lea las respuestas y escriba las preguntas.

1. Yes, a wasp has just stung me.
   _____?

2. Yes, the little boy clung to his mother.
   _____?

3. Yes, John wrung out the clothes yesterday.
   _____?

4. No, I did not stick a stamp on the letter.
   _____?

5. Yes, Sally hung the clothes out in the garden.
   _____?

6. Yes, I have stuck more magnets on the fridge.
   _____?

7. No, the washing machine does not wring the clothes automatically.
   _____?

Clasificación: AY, AID

Ejercicio 1. Rellene los huecos con la forma correcta del verbo en paréntesis.

1. I never _____ it would be easy. (say)
2. He _____ for the meal yesterday. (pay)
3. I always try _____ _____ my bills on time. (pay)
4. He _____ never _____ that. (say)
5. That hen _____ many eggs last year. (lay)
6. She always _____ her clothes out to dry. (lay)

Ejercicio 2. Responda a las preguntas con una frase completa.

1. Has she said something to him?
   Yes, she _____.
2. Have they paid the waiter?
   Yes, they _____.
3. Has Mary laid the clothes out to dry?
   No, she _____.
4. Does that hen lay many eggs?
   No, she _____.
5. Did you pay for the drinks?
   Yes, I _____.
6. Did he really say that?
   Yes, he _____.

Ejercicio 3. Lea las respuestas y escriba las preguntas.

1. Yes, he said something stupid.
   _____?
2. Yes, they paid too much for the meal.
   _____?
3. Yes, she laid her head on his shoulder.
   _____?
4. Yes, that hen has laid more than a dozen eggs.
   _____?
5. Yes, she always says that.
   _____?

6. No, I haven't paid the telephone bill yet.

_____?

Clasificación: IND, OUND

Ejercicio 1. Rellene los huecos con la forma correcta del verbo en paréntesis.
1. John wants _____ _____ a better job. (find)
2. Susan _____ _____ a great apartment. (find)
3. Peter _____ his teeth when he sleeps. (grind)
4. I like _____ _____ my own coffee. (grind)
5. He _____ the alarm clock before he went to bed. (wind)
6. The little boy likes _____ _____ up his toy boat. (wind)
7. The criminal _____ the employees during the bank robbery. (bind)
8. Mothers used _____ _____ their daughters' feet in China. (bind)

Ejercicio 2. Responda a las preguntas con una frase completa.
1. Did John find his keys?
   Yes, he _____.
2. Has Mary ground the coffee?
   No, she _____.
3. Did the little girl wind up the toy duck?
   Yes, she _____.
4. Did women bind their daughters' feet in China?
   Yes, women _____.
5. Does he grind his teeth at night?
   No, he _____.
6. Has the little boy found his mother?
   Yes, he _____.

Ejercicio 3. Lea las respuestas y escriba las preguntas.
1. Yes, I found twenty dollars on the street today.

_____?

2. Yes, he wound his watch this morning.

_____?

215

3. No, she doesn't grind her teeth when she's angry.

   _____?

4. No, I haven't ground the coffee yet.

   _____?

5. No, I didn't find what I was looking for.

   _____?

6. Yes, the soldiers bound the prisoners.

   _____?

Clasificación: ELL, OLD

Ejercicio 1. Rellene los huecos con la forma correcta del verbo en paréntesis.

1. John always _____ funny jokes. (tell)
2. She _____ him about her job interview. (tell)
3. Do you intend _____ _____ your parents? (tell)
4. Nostradamus _____ the Second World War. (foretell)
5. Gypsies often _____ the future. (foretell)
6. Susan wants _____ _____ her car. (sell)
7. They _____ the company last year. (sell)
8. The sales rep _____ _____ a lot of books lately. (sell)

Ejercicio 2. Responda a las preguntas con una frase completa.

1. Did the little boy tell the truth?
   Yes, he _____.
2. Has Susan sold her car?
   No, she _____.
3. Did Nostradamus foretell the Spanish civil war?
   Yes, he _____.
4. Does Alice always tell such bad jokes?
   Yes, she _____.
5. Has Peter told you about his new job?
   No, he _____.
6. Did they sell their apartment?
   Yes, they _____.

Ejercicio 3. Lea las respuestas y escriba las preguntas.

1. No, the government didn't tell many lies.

   _____?

2. Yes, the gypsy foretold the man's future.

   _____?

3. No, John hasn't sold his computer.

   _____?

4. Yes, that sales rep sells many books.

   _____?

5. Yes, astrologists foretell the future.

   _____?

6. Yes, she has told him the truth.

   _____?

7. Yes, he always tells me the same thing.

   _____?

8. Yes, they sold their car.

   _____?

Clasificación: STAND, STOOD

Ejercicio 1. Rellene los huecos con la forma correcta del verbo en paréntesis.

1. She _____ up when he entered the room. (stand)
2. John never _____ my jokes. (understand)
3. The little girl _____ everything I told her. (understand)
4. The army _____ the enemy's attack last week. (withstand)
5. The employees _____ _____ a lot of pressure lately. (withstand)
6. Tom doesn't like _____ _____ in line. (stand)

Ejercicio 2. Responda a las preguntas con una frase completa.

1. Has he withstood the pressure at work?
   No, he _____.
2. Does he understand English?
   No, he _____.
3. Did they stand in line to buy the tickets?
   Yes, they _____.

4. Did she understand what he said?

Yes, she _____.

5. Did the soldiers withstand the ambush?

Yes, they _____.

6. Has that man stood there for a long time?

No, he _____.

Ejercicio 3. Lea las respuestas y escriba las preguntas.

1. Yes, he understood everything she said.

_____?

2. Yes, she stood in line for an hour.

_____?

3. Yes, the soldiers have withstood the difficult conditions.

_____?

4. No, they don't understand Spanish.

_____?

5. Yes, he withstood the pressure from his boss.

_____?

6. No, the beggar doesn't stand on that corner every day.

_____?

Clasificación: OLD, ELD

Ejercicio 1. Rellene los huecos con la forma correcta del verbo en paréntesis.

1. Nobody likes _____ _____ heavy objects. (hold)
2. They always _____ hands when they walk on the street. (hold)
3. The government _____ a lot of taxes last year. (withhold)
4. The guards _____ the prisoner in custody last night. (hold)
5. The prophet said, "_____! The Messiah is coming." (behold)
6. Don Quixote _____ the windmills in the distance. (behold)

Ejercicio 2. Responda a las preguntas con una frase completa.

1. Did the little girl hold her mother's hand?

Yes, she _____.

2. Has the government withheld a lot of taxes this year?

No, it _____.

3. Does she always hold the tennis racket in her left hand?
   Yes, she _____.

4. Did Don Quixote behold the windmills?
   Yes, he _____.

5. Did the politician withhold comment on the disaster?
   Yes, he _____.

6. Did she hold the baby in her arms?
   No, she _____.

Ejercicio 3. Lea las respuestas y escriba las preguntas.
1. No, the prince had never beheld such a beautiful lady.

   _____?

2. Yes, the little boy always holds his mother's hand.

   _____?

3. No, the government didn't withhold many taxes last year.

   _____?

4. Yes, he withheld his opinion.

   _____?

5. Yes, the guards held the prisoner in custody.

   _____?

6. No, Don Quixote did not behold his comrade's alarm.

   _____?

Clasificación: I-E, ID o IT

Ejercicio 1. Rellene los huecos con la forma correcta del verbo en paréntesis.
1. He is always trying _____ _____ something. (hide)
2. That dog _____ a baby yesterday. (bite)
3. The teacher always _____ the students. (chide)
4. The economy _____ _____ into a recession recently. (slide)
5. The thief _____ the money he had stolen. (hide)
6. He always _____ his pipe with a match. (light)
7. Her eyes _____ up when he entered the room. (light)
8. The children _____ down the hill yesterday. (slide)

219

Ejercicio 2. Responda a las preguntas con una frase completa.
1. Did the police hide the evidence?
   Yes, they _____.
2. Do you always chide him for coming home late?
   No, I _____.
3. Have they lit the candles on the birthday cake?
   Yes, they _____.
4. Did the little boy slide down the sand dune?
   Yes, he _____.
5. Does that dog bite?
   No, it _____.
6. Has she hidden his birthday present?
   Yes, she _____.
7. Do they always light up that building at night?
   No, they _____.
8. Has the price of gold slid recently?
   Yes, it _____.

Ejercicio 3. Lea las respuestas y escriba las preguntas.
1. Yes, a mosquito has just bit me.
   _____?
2. Yes, he lit her cigarette for her.
   _____?
3. No, he didn't hide the present under the bed.
   _____?
4. Yes, the little girl slid on the ice.
   _____?
5. No, his wife does not chide him constantly.
   _____?
6. Yes, the dog bit the little boy.
   _____?
7. Yes, he always hides when guests arrive.
   _____?
8. Yes, they light up the cathedral at night.
   _____?

Clasificación: 0, 0

Ejercicio 1. Rellene los huecos con la forma correcta del verbo en paréntesis.

1. He _____ the Oscar for best actor last year. (win)
2. He doesn't like _____ _____ . (lose)
3. The little girl's eyes _____ when she saw her mother. (shine)
4. Jessica always _____ her keys. (lose)
5. I _____ up very early this morning. (wake)
6. The police _____ at the criminal. (shoot)
7. That man _____ just _____ the lottery. (win)
8. She usually _____ up very late. (wake)

Ejercicio 2. Responda a las preguntas con una frase completa.

1. Has she won a lot of prizes?
   Yes, she _____.
2. Did that team lose the match?
   Yes, it _____.
3. Does he usually wake up that early?
   No, he _____.
4. Did the police shoot at the demonstrators?
   Yes, they _____.
5. Does the sun always shine in Spain?
   No, the sun _____.
6. Have you lost your wallet?
   No, I _____.
7. Did Chris win the lottery?
   Yes, he _____.
8. Did she wake up in the middle of the night?
   Yes, she _____.

Ejercicio 3. Lea las respuestas y escriba las preguntas.

1. No, the bank robber did not shoot at the police.
   _____?

2. No, he hasn't lost his umbrella.
   _____?

3. Yes, he woke up at seven o'clock this morning.

    _____?

4. Yes, Real Madrid won the soccer match.

    _____?

5. Yes, her eyes shone when she opened the present.

    _____?

6. Yes, the socialists have won the elections.

    _____?

7. No, she does not always lose at card games.

    _____?

8. Yes, the noise woke up the baby.

    _____?

Clasificación: A, A

Ejercicio 1. Rellene los huecos con la forma correcta del verbo en paréntesis.
1. She always _____ on that chair. (sit)
2. John _____ a lot of books. (have)
3. He _____ dinner last night. (make)
4. She _____ in the waiting room for two hours. (sit)
5. I _____ _____ a lot of visitors lately. (have)
6. He doesn't like _____ _____ mistakes. (make)
7. Their business _____ a lot of money last year. (make)
8. I _____ lunch with my sister yesterday. (have)

Ejercicio 2. Responda a las preguntas con una frase completa.
1. Have you had lunch yet?
    No, I _____
2. Did your mother make that dress?
    Yes, she _____.
3. Does he usually sit on the floor?
    No, he _____.
4. Does she have a digital camera?
    Yes, she _____.
5. Has the student made any mistakes?
    No, she _____

6. Did the cat sit on the sofa?

Yes, it _____.

Ejercicio 3. Lea las respuestas y escriba las preguntas.

1. No, Sally has not had breakfast yet.

_____?

2. No, I don't have time to go to the bank.

_____?

3. Yes, they had a long vacation.

_____?

4. Yes, Peter has just sat on a needle.

_____?

5. Yes, the little girl sat on the bed.

_____?

6. Yes, my mother makes delicious brownies.

_____?

7. Yes, he made an effort to get there on time.

_____?

8. Yes, the students have made a lot of progress.

_____?

Segundo Grupo

Clasificación: IN, AN, UN

Ejercicio 1. Rellene los huecos con la forma correcta del verbo en paréntesis.

1. She always finishes what she _____. (begin)
2. He _____ too much last night. (drink)
3. The stone _____ to the bottom of the lake. (sink)
4. Cotton always _____. (shrink)

5. John _____ _____ many laps in the pool. (swim)
6. He likes _____ _____ in the shower. (sing)
7. The phone _____ and I answered it. (ring)
8. She _____ ten miles yesterday. (run)
9. My sister _____ _____ a yoga course. (begin)
10. The public toilet at the park _____ of urine the last time I was there. (stink)

Ejercicio 2. Responda a las preguntas con una frase completa.
1. Has he begun his new job yet?
   No, he _____.
2. Do his socks always stink?
   Yes, his socks _____.
3. Does Mary always drink that much?
   No, she _____.
4. Have you ever sung in a choir?
   No, I _____.
5. Did she run around the block?
   Yes, she _____.
6. Did the ship sink?
   Yes, it _____.
7. Did the phone ring this morning?
   No, it _____.
8. Did the clothes shrink in the wash?
   Yes, the clothes _____.
9. Does John swim every day?
   No, he _____.
10. Have they drunk all the wine?
    No, they _____.

Ejercicio 3. Lea las respuestas y escriba las preguntas.
1. Yes, the movie has just begun.
   _____?

2. No, his jeans didn't shrink in the wash.
   _____?

3. Yes, Jenny swam a mile yesterday.
   _____?

4. Yes, her heart sank when she heard the news.

   _____?

5. Yes, the mother sang the baby to sleep.

   _____?

6. No, Ann doesn't drink beer.

   _____?

7. Yes, someone has just rung the doorbell.

   _____?

8. Yes, the old man stank of whiskey.

   _____?

9. Yes, John ran to catch the bus.

   _____?

10. Yes, he runs ten miles every day.

   _____?

Clasificación: I-E, O-E, I-EN

Ejercicio 1. Rellene los huecos con la forma correcta del verbo en paréntesis.
   1. She _____ him a letter last month. (write)
   2. He _____ _____ since he was a teenager. (drive)
   3. John _____ his bicycle to work every day. (ride)
   4. The sun _____ at seven o'clock this morning. (rise)
   5. Alice always _____ to do her best. (strive)
   6. She got angry and _____ out of the room. (stride)
   7. He _____ _____ me many e-mails. (write)
   8. Mark wants _____ _____ across the United States. (drive)
   9. The little boy _____ from the table and left the room. (rise)
   10. I _____ never _____ a horse. (ride)

Ejercicio 2. Responda a las preguntas con una frase completa.
   1. Did she write him a letter?
      Yes, she _____.
   2. Does John usually drive to work?
      Yes, he _____.
   3. Has Alice always striven to do her best?
      Yes, she _____.

225

4. Did the man stride down the street?
   No, he _____.
5. Do you ride the subway often?
   No, I _____.
6. Have prices risen this year?
   Yes, prices _____.
7. Have you written to him lately?
   No, I _____.
8. Did he drive to the supermarket?
   Yes, he _____.

Ejercicio 3. Lea las respuestas y escriba las preguntas.
1. Yes, the teacher strode into the classroom.
   _____?
2. Yes, Sally always strives to get good grades.
   _____?
3. Yes, the price of gasoline rose a lot last year.
   _____?
4. No, she has not written many books.
   _____?
5. Yes, John drove to work this morning.
   _____?
6. No, Lucy has never ridden a bicycle.
   _____?
7. Yes, Sheila drives her children to school every day.
   _____?
8. Yes, he writes a lot of reports.
   _____?

Clasificación: E-A, O-E, O-EN

Ejercicio 1. Rellene los huecos con la forma correcta del verbo en paréntesis.
1. The president _____ at a press conference yesterday. (speak)
2. I _____ _____ to him many times. (speak)
3. Someone _____ just _____ my wallet. (steal)
4. Peter always _____ my pens. (steal)

5. John _____ his leg last year. (break)
6. The elevator _____ _____ down again. (break)
7. Mary is going _____ _____ a blanket. (weave)
8. She _____ _____ many beautiful blankets. (weave)
9. They _____ to go hiking last summer. (choose)
10. _____ you _____ the new curtains yet? (choose)
11. Water _____ at zero degrees Celsius. (freeze)
12. The snow _____ the crops last year. (freeze)

Ejercicio 2. Responda a las preguntas con una frase completa.
1. Have you ever spoken in public?
   No, I _____.
2. Does Mary speak Spanish?
   Yes, she _____.
3. Did the little boy steal the candy?
   Yes, he _____.
4. Has the computer broken down?
   No, it _____.
5. Did he break any rules?
   No, he _____.
6. Does Ann weave a lot of blankets?
   Yes, she _____.
7. Did he choose the blue shirt?
   Yes, he _____.
8. Has the snow frozen the crops?
   Yes, the snow _____.

Ejercicio 3. Lea las respuestas y escriba las preguntas.
1. No, he does not speak Chinese.
   _____?

2. Yes, John spoke to his sister yesterday.
   _____?

3. No, she did not steal my lighter.
   _____?

4. Yes, he always breaks the traffic regulations.
   _____?

5. Yes, Sally broke her arm last year.

   _____?

6. Yes, my friend wove that blanket.

   _____?

7. Yes, she chose the color of the walls.

   _____?

8. Yes, the government froze taxes last year.

   _____?

Clasificación: OW, EW, OWN

Sub-clasificación: AW, EW, AWN

Ejercicio 1. Rellene los huecos con la forma correcta del verbo en paréntesis.

1. I _____ _____ John for years. (know)
2. She _____ how to fly a plane when she was nineteen years old. (know)
3. Those plants _____ _____ a lot. (grow)
4. Mary _____ tomatoes in her backyard every year. (grow)
5. The little boy likes _____ _____ his toys everywhere. (throw)
6. He _____ _____ his clothes all over the floor. (throw)
7. She _____ him a kiss as she left. (blow)
8. The little girl wants _____ _____ up the balloon. (blow)
9. John _____ to Miami last week. (fly)
10. Eagles _____ very high. (fly)
11. Picasso _____ a lot when he was a child. (draw)
12. I _____ _____ my bank account. (overdraw)

Ejercicio 2. Responda a las preguntas con una frase completa.

1. Does Jane know how to ride a bicycle?
   Yes, she _____.
2. Have you known him for a long time?
   No, I _____.
3. Did you grow up in the United States?
   Yes, I _____.

4. Do people's noses grow when they tell lies?
   No, people's noses _____.
5. Did the little girl throw the ball?
   Yes, she _____.
6. Has she blown up the balloon?
   No, she _____.
7. Have you ever flown in a helicopter?
   No, I _____.
8. Did he fly to New York last week?
   No, he _____.
9. Did you draw that picture?
   No, I _____.
10. Did John withdraw money from the bank this morning?
    Yes, he _____.

Ejercicio 3. Lea las respuestas y escriba las preguntas.
1. Yes, she knows his parents.
   _____?
2. Yes, they knew each other when they were children.
   _____?
3. Yes, the grass has grown a lot this year.
   _____?
4. Yes, Alicia grew up in Mexico.
   _____?
5. No, he didn't throw the ball over the fence.
   _____?
6. Yes, the baby has thrown the food all over the floor.
   _____?
7. Yes, the little girl blew her mother a kiss.
   _____?
8. Yes, the hurricane has blown down many trees.
   _____?
9. Yes, Mark flew to Los Angeles last week.
   _____?
10. No, she does not fly home every week.
    _____?

11. Yes, the little boy drew a picture of a dog.

    _____?

12. Yes, he has withdrawn a lot of money from the bank.

    _____?

Clasificación: AKE, OOK, AKEN

Ejercicio 1. Rellene los huecos con la forma correcta del verbo en paréntesis.

1. She likes _____ _____ sugar with her coffee. (take)
2. They _____ _____ the dog to the vet. (take)
3. He _____ her for a movie star when he saw her. (mistake)
4. Sally always _____ the sugar for the salt. (mistake)
5. John _____ _____ many projects recently. (undertake)
6. The lawyer decided _____ _____ the case. (undertake)
7. They always _____ hands when they meet. (shake)
8. The building _____ during the earthquake. (shake)
9. Jesus said, "Father, why _____ you _____ me?" (forsake)
10. All her friends _____ _____ her. (forsake)

Ejercicio 2. Responda a las preguntas con una frase completa.

1. Have you ever taken a yoga course?
   No, I _____.
2. Did John take the garbage out?
   Yes, he _____.
3. Did Don Quixote mistake the windmills for giants?
   Yes, Don Quixote _____.
4. Have you ever mistaken a cat for a rabbit?
   No, I _____.
5. Has the lawyer undertaken the case?
   No, she _____.
6. Did you undertake the project?
   Yes, I _____.
7. Did his hands shake before the interview?
   Yes, his hands _____.
8. Did Judas forsake Jesus?
   Yes, Judas _____.

Ejercicio 3. Lea las respuestas y escriba las preguntas.

1. No, he didn't take her out to dinner.

_____?

2. Yes, she has taken my umbrella.

_____?

3. Yes, Peter mistook my jacket for his.

_____?

4. Yes, she always mistakes him for his twin brother.

_____?

5. Yes, the lawyer undertook the case.

_____?

6. Yes, John takes milk with his tea.

_____?

7. No, he hasn't shaken hands with the queen.

_____?

8. Yes, the little girl shook her head.

_____?

Clasificación: EAR, ORE, ORN

Ejercicio 1. Rellene los huecos con la forma correcta del verbo en paréntesis.

1. She always _____ big earrings. (wear)
2. I don't like _____ _____ a watch. (wear)
3. Tom _____ a tuxedo to the wedding yesterday. (wear)
4. After he read the letter, he _____ it up. (tear)
5. I _____ _____ my favorite jeans. (tear)
6. The little boy _____ that it was the truth. (swear)
7. He always _____ when he's angry. (swear)
8. She _____ pressure well. (bear)
9. The tree _____ a lot of apples last year. (bear)

Ejercicio 2. Responda a las preguntas con una frase completa.

1. Did you wear the pink dress to the party?
   No, I _____.
2. Does Mark wear glasses?
   No, he _____.

3. Have you ever worn a Scottish kilt?
   No, I _____.
4. Did the little girl tear her dress?
   No, she _____.
5. Did you tear up the letter?
   Yes, I _____.
6. Do you swear that it's true?
   Yes, I _____.
7. Has the witness sworn on the Bible?
   Yes, he _____.
8. Has that tree born a lot of fruit?
   No, it _____.

Ejercicio 3. Lea las respuestas y escriba las preguntas.
1. Yes, she always wears her sister's clothes.
   _____?
2. No, Mark has never worn that jacket.
   _____?
3. Yes, the thief wore a stocking over his head.
   _____?
4. Yes, he tore a muscle in his aerobics class.
   _____?
5. Yes, John has torn his favorite shirt.
   _____?
6. Yes, she swore it was the truth.
   _____?
7. Yes, that old man swears a lot.
   _____?
8. Yes, the lioness bore five cubs.
   _____?

Clasificación: I-E, A-E, I-EN

Ejercicio 1. Rellene los huecos con la forma correcta del verbo en paréntesis.
1. My boss is going _____ _____ me a bonus this year. (give)
2. He _____ his mother a big hug when she arrived. (give)

3. Susan _____ _____ a lot of money to charity this year. (give)
4. John never _____ her for leaving him. (forgive)
5. She _____ never _____ him for what he did. (forgive)
6. I _____ you to smoke in class. (forbid)
7. He _____ _____ his daughter to go out with that boy. (forbid)
8. He _____ his wife good-bye as he walked out the door. (bid)
9. What did he _____ you to do for him? (bid)

Ejercicio 2. Responda a las preguntas con una frase completa.
1. Does Susan give money to charity?
   Yes, she _____.
2. Have they given him a raise at work?
   No, they _____.
3. Did he give her a birthday present?
   No, he _____.
4. Has he forgiven you?
   Yes, he _____.
5. Did the little girl forgive her brother for hitting her?
   No, she _____.
6. Did the mother forbid her daughter to smoke?
   Yes, she _____.
7. Has he forbidden you to talk about it?
   Yes, he _____.
8. Has she bidden you to come to her party?
   Yes, she _____.

Ejercicio 3. Lea las respuestas y escriba las preguntas.
1. Yes, he gave her good advice.
   _____?
2. Yes, they give their old clothes to the church.
   _____?
3. Yes, she has given him a lot of money lately.
   _____?
4. No, she never forgave him.
   _____?

5. Yes, I forgive you.

_____?

6. Yes, she forbade him to talk about it.

_____?

7. Yes, the law forbids smoking in public places.

_____?

8. Yes, he bids his wife farewell before every business trip.

_____?

Clasificación: ET, OT, OTTEN

Sub-clasificación: EN (participio pasado)

Ejercicio 1. Rellene los huecos con la forma correcta del verbo en paréntesis.

1. Susan would like _____ _____ a new car. (get)
2. Steve always _____ what he wants. (get)
3. They _____ a new TV set yesterday. (get)
4. She never _____ a face. (forget)
5. I _____ _____ his name. (forget)
6. I _____ to call her yesterday. (forget)
7. The Virgin Mary _____ the baby Jesus. (beget)
8. He _____ in the same restaurant every day. (eat)
9. I _____ _____ too much. (eat)
10. The price of coffee _____ last year. (fall)

Ejercicio 2. Responda a las preguntas con una frase completa.

1. Has Tom gotten a new job?
   Yes, he _____.
2. Do you get the newspaper every day?
   No, I _____.
3. Has she ever forgotten his birthday?
   No, she _____.
4. Does he often forget things?
   Yes, he _____.
5. Does she eat a lot of junk food?
   No, she _____.

6. Have you eaten at this restaurant before?
   Yes, I _____.
7. Did the little boy fall off the bicycle?
   No, he _____.
8. Have airfares fallen recently?
   No, airfares _____.

Ejercicio 3. Lea las respuestas y escriba las preguntas.
1. Yes, Sally has gotten a new haircut.

   _____?
2. Yes, he got a digital camera last week.

   _____?
3. Yes, they forgot to take an umbrella.

   _____?
4. Yes, she always forgets people's names.

   _____?
5. No, he doesn't eat red meat.

   _____?
6. Yes, the cat ate the leftovers.

   _____?
7. Yes, the dollar has fallen against the euro lately.

   _____?
8. Yes, night falls earlier in the winter.

   _____?

Clasificación: OME, AME, OME

Ejercicio 1. Rellene los huecos con la forma correcta del verbo en paréntesis.
1. My friend would like _____ _____ to the party. (come)
2. She _____ never _____ to my house. (come)
3. They _____ to visit last year. (come)
4. Mark wants _____ _____ an anthropologist. (become)
5. He _____ _____ very impatient lately. (become)
6. Lula _____ president of Brazil in 2003. (become)
7. Susan _____ _____ many obstacles in her life. (overcome)
8. The little girl finally _____ her fear of the dark. (overcome)

Ejercicio 2. Responda a las preguntas con una frase completa.
1. Did John come to the party?
   No, he _____.
2. Have you come here before?
   No, I _____.
3. Does Mark come to visit often?
   Yes, he _____.
4. Does the little boy want to become a doctor?
   No, he _____.
5. Did Luis become a U.S. citizen?
   Yes, he _____.
6. Has Sally become rich?
   No, she _____.
7. Has he overcome his fear of heights?
   No, he _____.
8. Did he overcome her resistance?
   Yes, he _____.

Ejercicio 3. Lea las respuestas y escriba las preguntas.
1. Yes, I came here last week.
   _____?
2. Yes, he comes to this restaurant often.
   _____?
3. No, they have not come here many times.
   _____?
4. Yes, the employees became very angry.
   _____?
5. Yes, he became president last year.
   _____?
6. No, Sally does not become impatient easily.
   _____?
7. Yes, John overcame his fear of flying.
   _____?
8. Yes, they have overcome many obstacles.
   _____?

Clasificaciones: A, B, C (afinidad en el participio pasado solamente)

Ejercicio 1. Rellene los huecos con la forma correcta del verbo en paréntesis.

1. My cat loves _____ _____ in the sun. (lie)
2. She _____ on the sofa and fell asleep. (lie)
3. He _____ _____ often on this rock. (lie)
4. The soldiers _____ _____ many innocent people. (slay)
5. They _____ _____ friends for years. (be)
6. My parents _____ on vacation last week. (be)
7. They _____ both very obstinate. (be)
8. I _____ Sally yesterday. (see)
9. Tom _____ _____ that movie three times. (see)
10. Susan _____ _____ a lot of work today. (do)
11. He _____ the cooking yesterday. (do)
12. They _____ camping last weekend. (go)
13. Sally _____ to the gym every day. (go)
14. My uncle _____ _____ surgery several times. (undergo)

Ejercicio 2. Responda a las preguntas con una frase completa.

1. Does your dog always lie on that cushion?
   Yes, he _____.
2. Have you ever lain on a waterbed?
   No, I _____.
3. Did David slay Goliath?
   Yes, David _____.
4. Were you sick yesterday?
   No, I _____.
5. Has John been depressed lately?
   Yes, he _____.
6. Are you angry at him?
   No, I _____.
7. Do you see each other often?
   No, we _____.
8. Have you seen that movie?
   Yes, I _____.

9. Did you see the car accident?
   No, I _____.
10. Did the little boy do his homework?
   Yes, he _____.
11. Have they done a lot of traveling?
   No, they _____.
12. Did she go away last weekend?
   No, she _____.
13. Has John gone to lunch yet?
   No, he _____.
14. Did your father undergo surgery last week?
   Yes, he _____.

Ejercicio 3. Lea las respuestas y escriba las preguntas.
1. Yes, the students lay on the grass.

   _____?
2. Yes, the farmer has slain the pig.

   _____?
3. Yes, they have been to New York many times.

   _____?
4. Yes, she was very nervous before the interview.

   _____?
5. Yes, Ann sees her mother every week.

   _____?
6. Yes, Dorothy saw a shooting star.

   _____?
7. Yes, the wise man foresaw the disaster.

   _____?
8. No, the company doesn't do a lot of business overseas.

   _____?
9. Yes, John did well on the exam.

   _____?
10. Yes, they've gone out to dinner.

   _____?

11. Yes, his friends went to the concert.

_____?

12. Yes, the economy has undergone a major crisis.

_____?

Tercer Grupo

Clasificación: ET, ET, ET con variantes EAD y EAT

Ejercicio 1. Rellene los huecos con la forma correcta del verbo en paréntesis.
1. She always _____ him do what he wants. (let)
2. The teacher _____ the students leave early yesterday. (let)
3. He _____ never _____ me use his car. (let)
4. John _____ the alarm clock last night. (set)
5. The company needs _____ _____ new objectives. (set)
6. The little girl _____ her pants every day. (wet)
7. I _____ it will rain tomorrow. (bet)
8. She _____ a lot of money at the horse races yesterday. (bet)
9. Gossip always _____ quickly. (spread)
10. He sat down and _____ his legs. (spread)
11. I _____ a lot in my last aerobics class. (sweat)
12. France _____ Brazil in the 2002 World Soccer Cup. (beat)

Ejercicio 2. Responda a las preguntas con una frase completa.
1. Did John let her use his computer?
   Yes, he _____.
2. Has his boss let him take the day off work?
   No, his boss _____.
3. Did they set a time for the meeting?
   No, they _____.

4. Has the company set new objectives?

   No, it _____.

5. Did the rain wet all the clothes?

   Yes, it _____.

6. Did he bet all his money on that horse?

   No, he _____.

7. Has the epidemic spread very quickly?

   No, it _____.

8. Don't your feet sweat in those socks?

   No, they _____.

9. Has Zaragoza ever beat Real Madrid in a soccer match?

   Yes, Zaragoza _____.

10. Did John beat his brother playing cards?

   Yes, John _____.

Ejercicio 3. Lea las respuestas y escriba las preguntas.

1. No, she never lets her hair down.

   _____?

2. No, the police didn't let him cross the barrier.

   _____?

3. Yes, they've set a date for their next meeting.

   _____?

4. Yes, I always set objectives for myself.

   _____?

5. Yes, the little boy wet his bed last night.

   _____?

6. Yes, the rain wet all the laundry.

   _____?

7. No, he didn't bet on that horse.

   _____?

8. Yes, the rumor spread like wildfire.

   _____?

9. Yes, Ann sweats a lot at the gym.

   _____?

10. Yes, that man beats his wife.

   _____?

Clasificación: IT, IT, IT

Sub-clasificación: ID, ID, ID

Ejercicio 1. Rellene los huecos con la forma correcta del verbo en paréntesis.

1. The boy _____ his little sister yesterday. (hit)
2. That player _____ _____ the ball five times. (hit)
3. John _____ smoking last year. (quit)
4. The president's secretary _____ just _____. (quit)
5. That old man always _____ on the street. (spit)
6. The little girl got angry and _____ on her brother. (spit)
7. They decided _____ _____ the profits. (split)
8. John and Sally usually _____ the bill when they go out for dinner. (split)
9. He _____ too much at the auction yesterday. (bid)
10. She wants _____ _____ _____ of all her old clothes. (get rid)

Ejercicio 2. Responda a las preguntas con una frase completa.

1. Does Steffi Graf hit the ball hard?
   Yes, she _____.
2. Has that boy just hit you?
   Yes, he _____.
3. Have you quit smoking yet?
   No, I _____.
4. Did your sister quit her job?
   No, she _____.
5. Did that man just spit in front of you?
   Yes, he _____.
6. Have they split the profits between them?
   No, they _____.
7. Did they split the bill?
   Yes, they _____.
8. Have they bid on the same horse?
   No, they _____.

9. Did he bid on that painting?

   Yes, he _____.

10. Did Sally get rid of her old TV set?

    Yes, she _____.

Ejercicio 3. Lea las respuestas y escriba las preguntas.

1. No, he didn't hit the ball very hard.

   _____?

2. No, Billy has not hit his little sister twice today.

   _____?

3. Yes, Susan has quit several jobs.

   _____?

4. Yes, he quit drinking last year.

   _____?

5. Yes, he always spits in public places.

   _____?

6. Yes, the famous actress spit on the paparazzi.

   _____?

7. Yes, the company splits its profits among the shareholders.

   _____?

8. Yes, they always split the bill when they go out.

   _____?

9. No, the man did not bid $100 on the horse.

   _____?

10. Yes, she finally got rid of him.

    _____?

Clasificación: U-T u O-T

Ejercicio 1. Rellene los huecos con la forma correcta del verbo en paréntesis.

1. The little girl wanted _____ _____ the cake. (cut)
2. Lucy _____ her finger yesterday. (cut)
3. He _____ the door behind him when he left. (shut)
4. She always _____ the windows at night. (shut)
5. The matador _____ his sword into the bull. (thrust)
6. It _____ a lot of money to buy a house nowadays. (cost)

7. A gallon of gasoline _____ a lot less last year. (cost)
8. My back _____ _____ a lot lately. (hurt)
9. She didn't mean _____ _____ his feelings. (hurt)
10. The little boy _____ into the room unexpectedly. (burst)
11. I feel so full I think I'm going _____ _____. (burst)
12. My neighbor _____ just _____ his house up for sale. (put)

Ejercicio 2. Responda a las preguntas con una frase completa.
1. Did Tom cut himself on the bread knife?
   No, he _____.
2. Does your sister cut your hair?
   Yes, she _____.
3. Did you shut the front door?
   Yes, I _____.
4. Have they shut all the windows?
   No, they _____.
5. Has the matador thrust his sword into the bull?
   No, he _____.
6. Did your TV set cost a lot of money?
   No, it _____.
7. Does that car cost a lot?
   Yes, it _____.
8. Does your throat hurt?
   No, it _____.
9. Did the injection hurt a lot?
   Yes, it _____.
10. Did the little girl burst into tears?
    No, she _____.
11. Have you put your passport in a safe place?
    Yes, I _____.
12. Did he put the keys on the table?
    Yes, he _____.

Ejercicio 3. Lea las respuestas y escriba las preguntas.
1. Yes, he cut his finger on the sheet of paper.

   _____?

2. Yes, she always cuts out clippings from magazines.

   _____?

3. Yes, she shut her eyes during parts of the movie.

   _____?

4. No, he hasn't shut all the windows.

   _____?

5. Yes, the killer thrust the dagger into the man's heart.

   _____?

6. Yes, my computer cost a lot of money to repair.

   _____?

7. Yes, that wine costs over twenty dollars.

   _____?

8. Yes, he hurt his knee running.

   _____?

9. Yes, her rejection has hurt his pride.

   _____?

10. Yes, the little boy burst into tears suddenly.

    _____?

11. Yes, they have put their apartment up for sale.

    _____?

12. Yes, he put his arm around her.

    _____?

Clasificación: CAST, CAST, CAST

Ejercicio 1. Rellene los huecos con la forma correcta del verbo en paréntesis.

1. She _____ him an angry look when he arrived. (cast)
2. He _____ _____ a glance at the report. (cast)
3. That channel always _____ a lot of news programs. (broadcast)
4. He _____ the news that he was getting married. (broadcast)
5. The weather man _____ _____ rain for tomorrow. (forecast)
6. It is very difficult _____ _____ the stock market. (forecast)

Ejercicio 2. Responda a las preguntas con una frase completa.

1. Did the villagers cast stones at the soldiers?
   Yes, they _____.

2. Have you cast a glance at that report?
   No, I _____.

3. Have they forecast snow for the weekend?
   Yes, they _____.

4. Did the government forecast the economic crisis?
   No, it _____.

5. Did they broadcast the news on the radio?
   No, they _____.

6. Does he always broadcast his son's achievements?
   Yes, he _____.

Ejercicio 3. Lea las respuestas y escriba las preguntas.

1. Yes, he cast a quick look around the room.
   _____?

2. Yes, they have cast their votes.
   _____?

3. Yes, the radio broadcast the election results.
   _____?

4. No, they haven't broadcast the news yet.
   _____?

5. Yes, they have forecast a decline in real estate prices.
   _____?

6. No, they don't forecast rain for tomorrow.
   _____?

SOLUCIONES

Primer Grupo

Clasificación: OUGHT

Ejercicio 1. 1. to buy 2. brought 3. have thought 4. to seek 5. fought 6. Did (you) buy 7. seek 8. fought 9. to bring 10. Do (you) think

Ejercicio 2. 1. (Yes, she) bought a new car. 2. (No, I) haven't bought her a present. 3. (No, he) didn't fight in the war. 4. (Yes, she) sought some advice. 5. (Yes, I) have brought you that book. 6. (Yes, he) brought his friend to the party. 7. (No, I) haven't thought about it. 8. (Yes, he) thought of her yesterday.

Ejercicio 3. 1. When you were young, did you fight a lot with your brother? 2. Do John and Alice fight constantly? 3. Do you buy the newspaper every day? 4. Have you bought her a birthday present? 5. Did they bring many presents when they came? 6. Have you brought the book for me? 7. Do you think it's a good idea? 8. Have you thought about him a lot lately?

Clasificación: EE o EA, E-T

Ejercicio 1. 1. slept 2. to keep 3. Have (you) swept 4. wept 5. kept 6. met 7. have felt 8. left 9. sleep 10. Have (you ever) met

Ejercicio 2. 1. (No, I) didn't sleep well last night. 2. (Yes, he) kept the book. 3. (No, they) haven't swept the floor. 4. (No, I) haven't met your sister. 5. (Yes, they) left after the concert. 6. (No, we) haven't kept in contact. 7. (Yes, I) felt happy when I saw him. 8. (Yes, she) knelt during mass.

Ejercicio 3. 1. Did he sleep on the sofa last night? 2. Did they meet in Mexico? 3. Have they left? 4. Did you sweep the floor yesterday? 5. Did your mother weep at her brother's funeral? 6. Did you feel very tired last night? 7. Has your cat often crept up on you? 8. Have you always slept with the window open? 9. Did the little boy kneel before the queen? 10. Do you meet for coffee every morning?

Clasificación: EE o EA, E-T

Ejercicio 1. 1. deals 2. have (never) dealt 3. leapt 4. dwelt 5. leaps 6. meant 7. have meant 8. to leap

Ejercicio 2. 1. (No, I) have never dealt with him. 2. (Yes, she) meant what she said. 3. (No, my cat) doesn't always leap around the room. 4. (Yes, primitive man) dwelt in caves. 5. (Yes, I) deal with a lot of customers. 6. (Yes, the dolphins) leapt through the hoops.

Ejercicio 3. 1. Does modern man dwell in caves? 2. Does John always mean what he says? 3. Did the dog leap at you? 4. Did she mean to offend him? 5. Has Mary dealt with many important clients? 6. Has the cat leapt onto the sofa?

Clasificación: D, T

Ejercicio 1. 1. sent 2. has spent 3. to lend 4. lent 5. built 6. sent 7. to build 8. spent

Ejercicio 2. 1. (Yes, I) sent off the package. 2. (No, they) haven't built a new airport. 3. (Yes, he) spends a lot of money on books. 4. (No, they) haven't spent all the money. 5. (Yes, he) built that house. 6. (No, I) don't send a lot of e-mails. 7. (No, they) didn't lend me the money. 8. (Yes, he) lent me his car.

Ejercicio 3. 1. Did you lend John that book? 2. Did you spend a lot of time on that project? 3. Have they built a new museum? 4. Did she bend down to kiss the child? 5. Did Susan send you an e-mail last week? 6. Do they want to build a new park? 7. Does Mary always lend her sister money? 8. Has Tom spent a lot of money lately?

Clasificación: I, U

Ejercicio 1. 1. wrings 2. has hung 3. cling 4. clung 5. has (ever) stung 6. stung 7. stuck 8. to strike

Ejercicio 2. 1. (Yes, it) wrung the clothes. 2. (No, he) hasn't hung the painting. 3. (No, they) didn't sting me last night. 4. (Yes, it) clung to its mother. 5. (Yes, a bee) has stung me. 6. (Yes, she) stuck the labels on the folders. 7. (Yes, he) struck a match to light the fire. 8. (Yes, he) hung up on me.

Ejercicio 3. 1. Has a wasp just stung you? 2. Did the little boy cling to his mother? 3. Did John wring out the clothes yesterday? 4. Did you stick a stamp on the letter?

5. Did Sally hang the clothes out in the garden? 6. Have you stuck more magnets on the fridge? 7. Does the washing machine wring the clothes automatically?

Clasificación: AY, AID

Ejercicio 1. 1. said 2. paid 3. to pay 4. has (never) said 5. laid 6. lays

Ejercicio 2. 1. (Yes, she) has said something to him. 2. (Yes, they) have paid the waiter. 3. (No, she) hasn't laid the clothes out to dry. 4. (No, she) doesn't lay many eggs. 5. (Yes, I) paid for the drinks. 6. (Yes, he) really said that.

Ejercicio 3. 1. Did he say something stupid? 2. Did they pay too much for the meal? 3. Did she lay her head on his shoulder? 4. Has that hen laid more than a dozen eggs? 5. Does she always say that? 6. Have you paid the telephone bill yet?

Clasificación: IND, OUND

Ejercicio 1. 1. to find 2. has found 3. grinds 4. to grind 5. wound 6. to wind 7. bound 8. to bind

Ejercicio 2. 1. (Yes, he) found his keys. 2. (No, she) hasn't ground the coffee. 3. (Yes, she) wound up the toy duck. 4. (Yes, women) bound their daughters' feet in China. 5. (No, he) doesn't grind his teeth at night. 6. (Yes, he) has found his mother.

Ejercicio 3. 1. Did you find twenty dollars on the street today? 2. Did he wind his watch this morning? 3. Does she grind her teeth when she's angry? 4. Have you ground the coffee yet? 5. Did you find what you were looking for? 6. Did the soldiers bind the prisoners?

Clasificación: ELL, OLD

Ejercicio 1. 1. tells 2. told 3. to tell 4. foretold 5. foretell 6. to sell 7. sold 8. has sold

Ejercicio 2. 1. (Yes, he) told the truth. 2. (No, she) hasn't sold her car. 3. (Yes, he) foretold the Spanish civil war. 4. (Yes, she) always tells such bad jokes. 5. (No, he) hasn't told me about his new job. 6. (Yes, they) sold their apartment.

Ejercicio 3. 1. Did the government tell many lies? 2. Did the gypsy foretell the man's future? 3. Has John sold his computer? 4. Does that sales rep sell many books? 5. Do astrologists foretell the future? 6. Has she told him the truth? 7. Does he always tell you the same thing? 8. Did they sell their car?

Clasificación: STAND, STOOD

Ejercicio 1. 1. stood 2. understands 3. understood 4. withstood 5. have withstood 6. to stand

Ejercicio 2. 1. (No, he) hasn't withstood the pressure at work. 2. (No, he) doesn't understand English. 3. (Yes, they) stood in line to buy the tickets. 4. (Yes, she) understood what he said. 5. (Yes, they) withstood the ambush. 6. (No, he) hasn't stood there for a long time.

Ejercicio 3. 1. Did he understand everything she said? 2. Did she stand in line for an hour? 3. Have the soldiers withstood the difficult conditions? 4. Do they understand Spanish? 5. Did he withstand the pressure from his boss? 6. Does the beggar stand on that corner every day?

Clasificación: OLD, ELD

Ejercicio 1. 1. to hold 2. hold 3. withheld 4. held 5. Behold 6. beheld

Ejercicio 2. 1. (Yes, she) held her mother's hand. 2. (No, it) hasn't withheld a lot of taxes this year. 3. (Yes, she) always holds the tennis racket in her left hand. 4. (Yes, he) beheld the windmills. 5. (Yes, he) withheld comment on the disaster. 6. (No, she) didn't hold the baby in her arms.

Ejercicio 3. 1. Had the prince ever beheld such a beautiful lady? 2. Does the little boy always hold his mother's hand? 3. Did the government withhold many taxes last year? 4. Did he withhold his opinion? 5. Did the guards hold the prisoner in custody? 6. Did Don Quixote behold his comrade's alarm?

Clasificación: I-E, ID o IT

Ejercicio 1. 1. to hide 2. bit 3. chides 4. has slid 5. hid 6. lights 7. lit 8. slid

Ejercicio 2. 1. (Yes, they) hid the evidence. 2. (No, I) don't always chide him for coming home late. 3. (Yes, they) have lit the candles on the birthday cake. 4. (Yes, he) slid down the sand dune. 5. (No, it) doesn't bite. 6. (Yes, she) has hidden his birthday present. 7. (No, they) don't always light up that building at night. 8. (Yes, it) has slid recently.

Ejercicio 3. 1. Has a mosquito just bit you? 2. Did he light her cigarette for her? 3. Did he hide the present under the bed? 4. Did the little girl slide on the ice?

5. Does his wife chide him constantly? 6. Did the dog bite the little boy? 7. Does he always hide when guests arrive? 8. Do they light up the cathedral at night?

Clasificación: O, O

Ejercicio 1. 1. won 2. to lose 3. shone 4. loses 5. woke 6. shot 7. has (just) won 8. wakes

Ejercicio 2. 1. (Yes, she) has won a lot of prizes. 2. (Yes, it) lost the match. 3. (No, he) doesn't usually wake up that early. 4. (Yes, they) shot at the demonstrators. 5. (No, the sun) doesn't always shine in Spain. 6. (No, I) haven't lost my wallet. 7. (Yes, he) won the lottery. 8. (Yes, she) woke up in the middle of the night.

Ejercicio 3. 1. Did the bank robber shoot at the police? 2. Has he lost his umbrella? 3. Did he wake up at seven o'clock this morning? 4. Did Real Madrid win the soccer match? 5. Did her eyes shine when she opened the present? 6. Have the socialists won the elections? 7. Does she always lose at card games? 8. Did the noise wake up the baby?

Clasificación: A, A

Ejercicio 1. 1. sits 2. has 3. made 4. sat 5. have had 6. to make 7. made 8. had

Ejercicio 2. 1. (No, I) haven't had lunch yet. 2. (Yes, she) made that dress. 3. (No, he) doesn't usually sit on the floor. 4. (Yes, she) has a digital camera. 5. (No, she) hasn't made any mistakes. 6. (Yes, it) sat on the sofa.

Ejercicio 3. 1. Has Sally had breakfast yet? 2. Do you have time to go to the bank? 3. Did they have a long vacation? 4. Has Peter just sat on a needle? 5. Did the little girl sit on the bed? 6. Does your mother make delicious brownies? 7. Did he make an effort to get there on time? 8. Have the students made a lot of progress?

Segundo Grupo

Clasificación: IN, AN, UN

Ejercicio 1. 1. begins 2. drank 3. sank 4. shrinks 5. has swum 6. to sing 7. rang 8. ran 9. has begun 10. stank

Ejercicio 2. 1. (No, he) hasn't begun his new job yet. 2. (Yes, his socks) always stink. 3. (No, she) doesn't always drink that much. 4. (No, I) have never sung in a choir. 5. (Yes, she) ran around the block. 6. (Yes, it) sank. 7. (No, it) didn't ring this morning. 8. (Yes, the clothes) shrank in the wash. 9. (No, he) doesn't swim every day. 10. (No, they) haven't drunk all the wine.

Ejercicio 3. 1. Has the movie just begun? 2. Did his jeans shrink in the wash? 3. Did Jenny swim a mile yesterday? 4. Did her heart sink when she heard the news? 5. Did the mother sing the baby to sleep? 6. Does Ann drink beer? 7. Has someone just rung the doorbell? 8. Did the old man stink of whiskey? 9. Did John run to catch the bus? 10. Does he run ten miles every day?

Clasificación: I-E, O-E, I-EN

Ejercicio 1. 1. wrote 2. has driven 3. rides 4. rose 5. strives 6. strode 7. has written 8. to drive 9. rose 10. have (never) ridden

Ejercicio 2. 1. (Yes, she) wrote him a letter. 2. (Yes, he) usually drives to work. 3. (Yes, she) has always striven to do her best. 4. (No, he) didn't stride down the street. 5. (No, I) don't ride the subway often. 6. (Yes, prices) have risen this year. 7. (No, I) haven't written to him lately. 8. (Yes, he) drove to the supermarket.

Ejercicio 3. 1. Did the teacher stride into the classroom? 2. Does Sally always strive to get good grades? 3. Did the price of gasoline rise a lot last year? 4. Has she written many books? 5. Did John drive to work this morning? 6. Has Lucy ever ridden a bicycle? 7. Does Sheila drive her children to school every day? 8. Does he write a lot of reports?

Clasificación: E-A, O-E, O-EN

Ejercicio 1. 1. spoke 2. have spoken 3. has (just) stolen 4. steals 5. broke 6. has broken 7. to weave 8. has woven 9. chose 10. Have (you) chosen 11. freezes 12. froze

Ejercicio 2. 1. (No, I) have never spoken in public. 2. (Yes, she) speaks Spanish. 3. (Yes, he) stole the candy. 4. (No, it) has not broken down. 5. (No, he) didn't break any rules. 6. (Yes, she) weaves a lot of blankets. 7. (Yes, he) chose the blue shirt. 8. (Yes, the snow) has frozen the crops.

Ejercicio 3. 1. Does he speak Chinese? 2. Did John speak to his sister yesterday? 3. Did she steal your lighter? 4. Does he always break the traffic regulations? 5. Did

Sally break her arm last year? 6. Did your friend weave that blanket? 7. Did she choose the color of the walls? 8. Did the government freeze taxes last year?

Clasificación: OW, EW, OWN

Sub-clasificación: AW, EW, AWN

Ejercicio 1. 1. have known 2. knew 3. have grown 4. grows 5. to throw 6. has thrown 7. blew 8. to blow 9. flew 10. fly 11. drew 12. have overdrawn

Ejercicio 2. 1. (Yes, she) knows how to ride a bicycle. 2. (No, I) haven't known him for a long time. 3. (Yes, I) grew up in the United States. 4. (No, people's noses) don't grow when they tell lies. 5. (Yes, she) threw the ball. 6. (No, she) hasn't blown up the balloon. 7. (No, I) have never flown in a helicopter. 8. (No, he) didn't fly to New York last week. 9. (No, I) didn't draw that picture. 10. (Yes, he) withdrew money from the bank this morning.

Ejercicio 3. 1. Does she know his parents? 2. Did they know each other when they were children? 3. Has the grass grown a lot this year? 4. Did Alicia grow up in Mexico? 5. Did he throw the ball over the fence? 6. Has the baby thrown the food all over the floor? 7. Did the little girl blow her mother a kiss? 8. Has the hurricane blown down many trees? 9. Did Mark fly to Los Angeles last week? 10. Does she fly home every week? 11. Did the little boy draw a picture of a dog? 12. Has he withdrawn a lot of money from the bank?

Clasificación: AKE, OOK, AKEN

Ejercicio 1. 1. to take 2. have taken 3. mistook 4. mistakes 5. has undertaken 6. to undertake 7. shake 8. shook 9. have (you) forsaken 10. have forsaken

Ejercicio 2. 1. (No, I) have never taken a yoga course. 2. (Yes, he) took the garbage out. 3. (Yes, Don Quixote) mistook the windmills for giants. 4. (No, I) have never mistaken a cat for a rabbit. 5. (No, she) hasn't undertaken the case. 6. (Yes, I) undertook the project. 7. (Yes, his hands) shook before the interview. 8. (Yes, Judas) forsook Jesus.

Ejercicio 3. 1. Did he take her out to dinner? 2. Has she taken your umbrella? 3. Did Peter mistake your jacket for his? 4. Does she always mistake him for his twin brother? 5. Did the lawyer undertake the case? 6. Does John take milk with his tea? 7. Has he shaken hands with the queen? 8. Did the little girl shake her head?

Clasificación: EAR, ORE, ORN

Ejercicio 1. 1. wears 2. to wear 3. wore 4. tore 5. have torn 6. swore 7. swears 8. bears 9. bore

Ejercicio 2. 1. (No, I) didn't wear the pink dress to the party. 2. (No, he) doesn't wear glasses. 3. (No, I) have never worn a Scottish kilt. 4. (No, she) didn't tear her dress. 5. (Yes, I) tore up the letter. 6. (Yes, I) swear that it's true. 7. (Yes, he) has sworn on the Bible. 8. (No, it) hasn't born a lot of fruit.

Ejercicio 3. 1. Does she always wear her sister's clothes? 2. Has Mark ever worn that jacket? 3. Did the thief wear a stocking over his head? 4. Did he tear a muscle in his aerobics class? 5. Has John torn his favorite shirt? 6. Did she swear it was the truth? 7. Does that old man swear a lot? 8. Did the lioness bear five cubs?

Clasificación: I-E, A-E, I-EN

Ejercicio 1. 1. to give 2. gave 3. has given 4. forgave 5. has (never) forgiven 6. forbid 7. has forbidden 8. bade 9. bid

Ejercicio 2. 1. (Yes, she) gives money to charity. 2. (No, they) haven't given him a raise at work. 3. (No, he) didn't give her a birthday present. 4. (Yes, he) has forgiven me. 5. (No, she) didn't forgive her brother for hitting her. 6. (Yes, she) forbade her daughter to smoke. 7. (Yes, he) has forbidden me to talk about it. 8. (Yes, she) has bidden me to come to her party.

Ejercicio 3. 1. Did he give her good advice? 2. Do they give their old clothes to the church? 3. Has she given him a lot of money lately? 4. Did she ever forgive him? 5. Do you forgive me? 6. Did she forbid him to talk about it? 7. Does the law forbid smoking in public places? 8. Does he bid his wife farewell before every business trip?

Clasificación: ET, OT, OTTEN

Sub-clasificación: EN (participio pasado)

Ejercicio 1. 1. to get 2. gets 3. got 4. forgets 5. have forgotten 6. forgot 7. begot 8. eats 9. have eaten 10. fell

Ejercicio 2. 1. (Yes, he) has gotten a new job. 2. (No, I) don't get the newspaper every day. 3. (No, she) has never forgotten his birthday. 4. (Yes, he) often forgets things. 5. (No, she) doesn't eat a lot of junk food. 6. (Yes, I) have eaten at this restaurant before. 7. (No, he) didn't fall off the bicycle. 8. (No, airfares) haven't fallen recently.

Ejercicio 3. 1. Has Sally gotten a new haircut? 2. Did he get a digital camera last week? 3. Did they forget to take an umbrella? 4. Does she always forget people's names? 5. Does he eat red meat? 6. Did the cat eat the leftovers? 7. Has the dollar fallen against the euro lately? 8. Does night fall earlier in the winter?

Clasificación: OME, AME, OME

Ejercicio 1. 1. to come 2. has (never) come 3. came 4. to become 5. has become 6. became 7. has overcome 8. overcame

Ejercicio 2. 1. (No, he) didn't come to the party. 2. (No, I) haven't come here before. 3. (Yes, he) comes to visit often. 4. (No, he) doesn't want to become a doctor. 5. (Yes, he) became a U.S. citizen. 6. (No, she) hasn't become rich. 7. (No, he) hasn't overcome his fear of heights. 8. (Yes, he) overcame her resistance.

Ejercicio 3. 1. Did you come here last week? 2. Does he come to this restaurant often? 3. Have they come here many times? 4. Did the employees become very angry? 5. Did he become president last year? 6. Does Sally become impatient easily? 7. Did John overcome his fear of flying? 8. Have they overcome many obstacles?

Clasificaciones: A, B, C (afinidad en el participio pasado solamente)

Ejercicio 1. 1. to lie. 2. lay 3. has lain 4. have slain 5. have been 6. were 7. are 8. saw 9. has seen 10. has done 11. did 12. went 13. goes 14. has undergone

Ejercicio 2. 1. (Yes, he) always lies on that cushion. 2. (No, I) have never lain on a waterbed. 3. (Yes, David) slew Goliath. 4. (No, I) wasn't sick yesterday. 5. (Yes, he) has been depressed lately. 6. (No, I) am not angry at him. 7. (No, we) don't see each other often. 8. (Yes, I) have seen that movie. 9. (No, I) didn't see the car accident. 10. (Yes, he) did his homework. 11. (No, they) haven't done a lot of traveling. 12. (No, she) didn't go away last weekend. 13. (No, he) hasn't gone to lunch yet. 14. (Yes, he) underwent surgery last week.

Ejercicio 3. 1. Did the students lie on the grass? 2. Has the farmer slain the pig? 3. Have they been to New York many times? 4. Was she very nervous before the interview? 5. Does Ann see her mother every week? 6. Did Dorothy see a shooting star? 7. Did the wise man foresee the disaster? 8. Does the company do a lot of business overseas? 9. Did John do well on the exam? 10. Have they gone out to dinner? 11. Did his friends go to the concert? 12. Has the economy undergone a major crisis?

Tercer Grupo

Clasificación: ET, ET, ET con variantes EAD y EAT

Ejercicio 1. 1. lets 2. let 3. has (never) let 4. set 5. to set 6. wets 7. bet 8. bet 9. spreads 10. spread 11. sweat 12. beat

Ejercicio 2. 1. (Yes, he) let her use his computer. 2. (No, his boss) hasn't let him take the day off work. 3. (No, they) didn't set a time for the meeting. 4. (No, it) hasn't set new objectives. 5. (Yes, it) wet all the clothes. 6. (No, he) didn't bet all his money on that horse. 7. (No, it) hasn't spread very quickly. 8. (No, they) don't sweat in these socks. 9. (Yes, Zaragoza) has beat Real Madrid in a soccer match. 10. (Yes, John) beat his brother playing cards.

Ejercicio 3. 1. Does she ever let her hair down? 2. Did the police let him cross the barrier? 3. Have they set a date for their next meeting? 4. Do you always set objectives for yourself? 5. Did the little boy wet his bed last night? 6. Did the rain wet all the laundry? 7. Did he bet on that horse? 8. Did the rumor spread like wildfire? 9. Does Ann sweat a lot at the gym? 10. Does that man beat his wife?

Clasificación: IT, IT, IT

Sub-clasificación: ID, ID, ID

Ejercicio 1. 1. hit 2. has hit 3. quit 4. has (just) quit 5. spits 6. spit 7. to split 8. split 9. bid 10. to get rid

Ejercicio 2. 1. (Yes, she) hits the ball hard. 2. (Yes, he) has just hit me. 3. (No, I) haven't quit smoking yet. 4. (No, she) didn't quit her job. 5. (Yes, he) just spit in front of me. 6. (No, they) haven't split the profits between them. 7. (Yes, they) split the bill. 8. (No, they) haven't bid on the same horse. 9. (Yes, he) bid on that painting. 10. (Yes, she) got rid of her old TV set.

Ejercicio 3. 1. Did he hit the ball very hard? 2. Has Billy hit his little sister twice today? 3. Has Susan quit several jobs? 4. Did he quit drinking last year? 5. Does he always spit in public places? 6. Did the famous actress spit on the paparazzi? 7. Does the company split its profits among the shareholders? 8. Do they always split the bill when they go out? 9. Did the man bid $100 on the horse? 10. Did she finally get rid of him?

Clasificación: U-T u O-T

Ejercicio 1. 1. to cut 2. cut 3. shut 4. shuts 5. thrust 6. costs 7. cost 8. has hurt 9. to hurt 10. burst 11. to burst 12. has (just) put

Ejercicio 2. 1. (No, he) didn't cut himself on the bread knife. 2. (Yes, she) cuts my hair. 3. (Yes, I) shut the front door. 4. (No, they) haven't shut all the windows. 5. (No, he) hasn't thrust his sword into the bull. 6. (No, it) didn't cost a lot of money. 7. (Yes, it) costs a lot. 8. (No, it) doesn't hurt. 9. (Yes, it) hurt a lot. 10. (No, she) didn't burst into tears. 11. (Yes, I) have put my passport in a safe place. 12. (Yes, he) put the keys on the table.

Ejercicio 3. 1. Did he cut his finger on the sheet of paper? 2. Does she always cut out clippings from magazines? 3. Did she shut her eyes during parts of the movie? 4. Has he shut all the windows? 5. Did the killer thrust the dagger into the man's heart? 6. Did your computer cost a lot of money to repair? 7. Does that wine cost over twenty dollars? 8. Did he hurt his knee running? 9. Has her rejection hurt his pride? 10. Did the little boy burst into tears suddenly? 11. Have they put their apartment up for sale? 12. Did he put his arm around her?

Clasificación: CAST, CAST, CAST

Ejercicio 1. 1. cast 2. has cast 3. broadcasts 4. broadcast 5. has forecast 6. to forecast

Ejercicio 2. 1. (Yes, they) cast stones at the soldiers. 2. (No, I) haven't cast a glance at that report. 3. (Yes, they) have forecast snow for the weekend. 4. (No, it) didn't forecast the economic crisis. 5. (No, they) didn't broadcast the news on the radio. 6. (Yes, he) always broadcasts his son's achievements.

Ejercicio 3. 1. Did he cast a quick look around the room? 2. Have they cast their votes? 3. Did the radio broadcast the election results? 4. Have they broadcast the news yet? 5. Have they forecast a decline in real estate prices? 6. Do they forecast rain for tomorrow?